The Millionaire Real Estate Mogul

I0391347

Strategies to Building Wealth with Real Estate

The information provided herein is stated to be truthful and consistent, in that any liability, in terms of inattention or otherwise, by any usage or abuse of any policies, processes, or directions contained within is the solitary and utter responsibility of the recipient reader. Under no circumstances will any legal responsibility or blame be held against the publisher for any reparation, damages, or monetary loss due to the information herein, either directly or indirectly.

Respective authors own all copyrights not held by the publisher.

The information herein is offered for informational purposes solely, and is universal as so. The presentation of the information is without contract or any type of guarantee assurance.

The trademarks that are used are without any consent, and the publication of the trademark is without permission or backing by the trademark owner. All trademarks and brands within this book are for clarifying purposes only and are the owned by the owners themselves, not affiliated with this document.

Table of Contents

Introduction

I want to thank you and congratulate you for purchasing the book, "*The Millionaire Real Estate Mogul: Strategies to Building Wealth with Real Estate.*"

This book contains proven steps and strategies on how to build your own real estate portfolio. It will teach you the basics of investing, financial analysis, risk analysis, and other aspects of owning real estate properties. By reading this eBook, you'll arm yourself with effective and practical tools that you can use to build wealth.

This book is for both the novice real estate investor and the experienced real estate investor. Anyone reading this book will learn something new that they didn't already know.

Again, congratulations on taking the steps to improve your real estate knowledge by purchasing this book. The fact that you have taken this step shows that you are determined and dedicated in your real estate endeavors, in which I give you my utmost respect.

Enjoy!

Chapter 1: Real Estate Investing – The Basics

Why invest in real estate? Well, expert investors consider real estate as the best way to gain wealth. It has created more millionaires than other forms of investments. Based on recent studies, many people will encounter financial problems by the time they retire. You have several assets to choose from. But real estate properties are your best bet if you want to secure financial stability for you and your family.

Most investors focus on stocks, bonds, options, savings accounts, and certificates of deposits. These options are safe. However, the numbers they return are not enough for accumulating wealth. In addition, inflation typically outperforms the profits from the said financial instruments. Here's an interesting point: how many people have become millionaires through their savings accounts? You can get exciting profits from stock investments. But the returns are not guaranteed. Stocks provide minimal tax advantages, and you are at the mercy of the companies you will invest in.

Real estate properties have better returns than other assets. In the U.S., the values of most properties quadrupled from the 50s to 2009. Although it is true that real estate has experienced ups and downs, it has a long history of continuous appreciation. Housing markets (e.g. in the U.S.) suffered from unusual corrections in the past, but real estate can recover and continue to dominate the list of profitable investment options.

The Pros of Real Estate

Leverage

This is the main reason why real estate is better than other assets (e.g. bonds, stocks, mutual funds, etc.). With leverage, you can acquire a lot of real estate properties without spending much.

For instance, you can buy a $200,000 real estate property by making a down payment of $40,000 (i.e. 20% of the total). Some properties even allow a ten-percent down payment, which gives you more leverage. Let's say you invested your $40,000 in the stock market. If your stock portfolio went up by 10% after one year, your assets will be $44,000.

Investing that same amount of money on a real estate property is more profitable. Let's assume that you invested $40,000 on a $400,000 house and that the value of the property went up by 10%. Here, the property will be worth $440,000. That means you will gain a whopping $40,000 profit (an increase of 100% over your initial investment).

Tax Advantages

With "investment properties", you can reduce your income tax by deducting the repair costs, depreciation, maintenance, insurance, mortgage interest, professional fees, etc. These deductions are separate from those of your residential properties. Current tax laws allow you to deduct the said expenses on all of your income-generating properties.

Important Note: Deductions for personal residence are limited to two properties.

Appreciation

The average value of real estate properties has increased continuously for more than 80 years. Market downturns occurred but the trend is always pointing upwards. This upward trend results from the laws of demand and supply. Humans have a never-ending demand for real estate - for shelter, for work (i.e. office space), for entertainment, etc. In addition, real estate properties benefit from inflation. The value of a real estate property increases when inflation is high.

Financing

Most assets require cash investments. For example, you must part with your own money in order to buy stocks. Trading stocks "on margin" is possible, but it is subject to the broker's limits and margin recall. Real estate properties, on the other hand, allow you to work with financiers. Lenders are willing to fund 80% to 90% of a property's market value.

Cash Flow

An investment property can generate positive cash flows for its owner. The cash flow of a property may vary because of different variables (e.g. market rent, down payment value, purchase price, related costs, etc.).

Acquiring a property properly means securing a great investment for you and your family. This type of investment can create a continuous stream of income for many years (or even decades). In general, you should look for properties with neutral or positive cash flows. Don't purchase a property with a negative cash flow, unless it allows you to "defer" a significant part of the down payment.

Tenants Will Pay the Mortgage

This is an attractive benefit that you can gain from real estate properties. You can buy a property and rent it out to other people. These individuals will pay rent each month - you can use their payments to take care of your mortgage. Basically, the tenants will purchase the property on your behalf.

How to Obtain Money for Down Payment

Real estate can help you build wealth quickly and easily. However, it requires an initial investment. In this part of the book, you'll learn about the ideal methods for collecting "down payment funds".

Important Note: In most cases, a lender will require you to pay 20% of the property's value as down payment. This percentage gives an acceptable protection in case a buyer defaults on the loan. This equity also prevents additional insurance premiums on your mortgage. Many people consider 20% as the standard down payment. But real estate investors are increasing their leverage by making low down payments. This strategy minimizes their initial capital but increases the resulting monthly costs (e.g. mortgage payments).

The list given below shows some of the best fund sources for your down payment:

- Savings - Most investors consider this as the best source of funds. If you want to attain financial freedom, you should save and invest your money in income-generating assets.

- 401(k) - You can utilize your 401(k) to obtain sufficient down payment. Pay it back with interest over a 5-year period. This fund source comes with pros and cons. Money lenders don't consider it as a debt while evaluating a person's debt-to-income ratio. Its main drawback is that it requires a payment within 90 days in case you resign or get terminated from your job. The 90-day timeframe will run the day after your official separation from your employer.

- IRA - This fund source can help you secure financial freedom for your retirement. It offers great return rates (especially over the long term). You may also use it without paying taxes, depending on the IRA you are using.

- Credit Lines - A business credit line can serve as an excellent fund source for your real estate investments. Each credit line can give you up to $100,000, and is available at low-interest rates. Use it if the property you want to buy involves extra monthly payments. Analyze the numbers first before utilizing this fund source since you will borrow money from financial institutions.

- Partners - You don't have to purchase real estate properties on your own. If you lack the funds, look for a person who wants to become an investor. Discuss your plan and see if he would be interested in establishing a partnership with you. Combine your funds, purchase a property, and divide the equity based on the capital you invested. Use the same ratio in dividing your profits. Talk to a lawyer or business consultant when preparing your "articles of partnership".

- Budget Control - Spend your money wisely if you want to build wealth. Many people claim that they don't have enough funds to invest, but keep on spending money on useless stuff. It's possible that your current income is enough to save up for your real estate investments. List down all of your expenses and cross out the unnecessary ones. The amount that you will be able to save might surprise you.

Chapter 2: How to Purchase a Rental Property

Rental properties can generate continuous streams of income quickly and securely. Unfortunately, it requires unusual knowledge from real estate investors. Although rental properties are unique, they share some similarities with personal properties. In this chapter, you'll learn how to purchase rental properties for your real estate portfolio.

First Step: Research

Many investors ignore this step. After deciding that they want to purchase rental properties, they'll just pay for the first property they'll see. In fact, they even spend more time choosing paint colors than learning more about the type of property they will acquire.

Here are the major benefits of researching:

- You will understand how rental systems work in the field of real estate.
- You will know the required budget.
- You will discover the type of neighborhood to focus on.
- You will know the range of rent payments in your chosen location.
- You will have a clear idea regarding the resulting ROI.

Second Step: Formulate a Strategy

Analyze the information you collected from the previous step. That information can help you build a plan for your real estate portfolio (you'll learn more about plans and strategies later). It would be best if you will write down your strategy and objectives, and review them regularly. These pieces of data can help you avoid distractions. For example, you won't get distracted by the house with an awesome pool that costs $350,000 if your chosen price range is $200,000 to $300,000.

Third Step: Choose Criteria

Real estate properties have different characteristics. Buying a property without detailed examination is a huge mistake. You can streamline your buying process by setting criteria for properties that you would like to buy. This way, you won't have to rely on your intuition while searching for potential investments.

While establishing the criteria, you have a lot of factors to choose from. Almost all investors consider price and location as important factors. You may follow the trend, or put emphasis on other factors. It's up to you. Just make sure that your chosen aspects match your strategy and objectives.

Fourth Step: Secure Financing

Inexperienced investors tend to search for great real estate properties before securing financing. Unfortunately, this tendency has caused pain and disappointment to people who can't afford the property they want. Although it usually happens to home buyers, people who buy rental properties can also suffer from it.

Talk to your bank and check all the funds available to you. Use the information you will collect in choosing the right price range. There are several financing options for real estate investors. Check these options and select the one that matches your strategy.

Fifth Step: Look for Available Properties

This is the most exciting part of the process. Today, you can find excellent rental properties in a number of ways. You may start your search by running an online query or talking to a broker/agent.

Websites can help you find properties quickly and easily. However, they don't have all the information you need. Additionally, online listings are not always updated. That means you still need to talk to a reputable real estate agent to obtain more information. The seller will pay for the agent's services once the property is sold - buyers can talk to agents for free.

Agents differ in terms of the properties they focus on. It would be best if you'll work with agents who concentrate on investment properties. These people can help you find great properties and secure profits. Share your criteria with the agent to make sure that his suggestions match your needs.

Sixth Step: Submit Your Offer

Make an offer once you find a property that matches your criteria. The agent will help you with this step. He will prepare the forms according to your demands and send them to a selling agent. Negotiations will start once the seller receives your offer.

Keep in mind that you are buying the property to make money. Thus, you can't spend too much regardless of how awesome the property looks. If you have a detailed plan, you'll know the type of cash flow you need. Never allow your emotions to affect your investment decisions. There will be times when you must walk away from a "perfect property" because of unfavorable negotiations. It is better to let go of a property than acquire it and face undesirable consequences.

You also need to remember that price is just one of the considerations. Here are other factors that you should analyze:

- Financing Contingency

- Inspection Contingency

- Closing Date

- Financial Concessions of the Seller

Seventh Step: Inspect the Property

At this point, both parties have agreed on the closing date and the total price. This is the perfect time for you to hire a professional inspector and check the condition of the property. The inspector will look for defects that can lead to future expenses. If there are significant issues, you may request for renegotiations. Make sure that you will submit this request within the "inspection contingency" period you indicated in your initial offer.

It's not a good idea to use a nickel-and-dime approach, especially if the property has an excellent value. There's always a risk that the seller will stop the transaction and sell the property to another buyer. However, you should protect yourself from properties that have huge (and expensive) problems. Analyze your options carefully and choose the ones that match your goals.

Important Note: This is also the period where you will finalize the arrangements with your lender. Once the closing day comes, you will receive the keys for your new property.

Eighth Step: Rent Out the Property

This is the final step of the process. Now, you are the landlord of a rental property. You must look for tenants in order to generate income. You will learn more about this in the next chapter.

Chapter 3: How to Rent Out a Property

Do you want to receive calls at 2am, delayed payments, and expensive evictions? No, you probably don't.

Landlords don't want any of the problems listed above. Unfortunately, many landlords suffer from the said issues.

According to real estate experts, these problems appear because landlords handled the "rent out process" incorrectly. Investors often underestimate the importance of getting a property rented. They take it for granted. You can prevent future headaches by implementing an intelligent approach in the renting process.

Your goal is to build wealth using your real estate portfolio. That means you need to handle your rental properties correctly. In this chapter, you'll find various tips, tricks, and strategies that you can use in renting out your real estate properties.

Renting a House - The Questions You Must Answer

You need to make some decisions before handing your keys to a tenant. Experts claim that these "pre-operating decisions" have a huge effect on the profits (or problems) that you will get. Answer the following questions before searching for potential tenants:

Should You Rent the Property?

In general, renting is better than selling. Here are the main reasons why:

- Renting allows you to turn a liability into an asset - For example, mortgaged properties are liabilities since they require you to make payments. By renting a mortgaged property, you can use it to pay the mortgage fees (or even make profits).

- Renting lets you keep the property - Real estate properties gain in value as years go by. That means you can benefit from holding a property for a long time. Selling a property, on the other hand, means quick funds but zero profits in the future. By renting a property, you can open a new source of revenue while waiting for a perfect time to put the house on sale.

- Renting helps you build wealth without spending much money - You already own the house, so costs (if any) will be minimal. Countless investors have used the renting route to achieve their dream of financial freedom.

- Renting allows you to use the property in the future - You will retain the ownership of the property, regardless of how long your tenants will stay in it. That means you will have an available house to live in if you'll need a shelter in the future.

Do You Have to Improve the Property First?

As the owner, you have a natural desire to enhance the property. If a property is in a great condition, finding tenants will be easy. The main issue lies in finding the appropriate condition of a property before renting it out. In most cases, you can rent out a property as long as it is clean and free from serious damages. It would be best if you'll get the services of professional cleaners before showing the house to potential tenants.

Are You Going to Manage the Property?

This question affects your entire business model. Do you want to manage the rental property or get the services of another person? In general, property managers charge 10% to 15% of the monthly fees. You also need to give them 50% of the initial rental payment whenever new tenants move in. Property managers take care of the following tasks:

- Handle evictions (you will pay the attorney's fees, though)
- Issue notices
- Monitor the property's finances
- Collect rents
- Look for new tenants

What is the Appropriate Rental Fee?

In real estate, you don't have much control over the amount of rents. The market will set that number for you.

Owners of rental properties aim for fair market rents, or the amount of money that tenants are willing to pay in your respective market.

This task requires extensive knowledge about your market. Search for rental properties with the same size, condition, and location as your own property. Use their rental amounts as a basis for determining the right rental fee.

Here are some resources that you can use to gain the necessary data:

- www.zillow.com
- www.trulia.com
- www.craigslist.org
- www.padmapper.com
- Local newspaper

Pose as an interested tenant and talk to different landlords. Look for properties that are comparable to yours and find their listed rate. This way, you'll know the correct rate for your rental house.

Finding the Best Tenants

Tenants play a huge role in the success of your rental business. Bad tenants will give you long periods of headaches and lost revenues. Great tenants, on the other hand, will give you long periods of peace and financial security. Unfortunately, landlords underestimate the importance of finding excellent tenants. This tendency often results in serious problems and missed earning opportunities.

Here's a step-by-step guide on how to find the best tenants:

First Step: Advertise

Your first objective is to get a large pool of tenants. This way, you'll have a high chance of finding excellent ones. Landlords use the following methods of advertising:

- Yard Signs - This is a traditional way of advertising. Despite its age, it can still attract many tenants.
- Newspaper Ads - This advertising strategy is old and expensive. However, it remains as one of the most effective ways to notify people about market offerings.
- Craigslist - Craigslist is a website that allows you to offer stuff online. You can use it to sell cars, computers, smartphones, etc. These days, landlords are also using this site to advertise their rental properties. Promoting your property here doesn't cost anything.

Second Step: Filter the Tenants

Filter the tenant's right after talking to them. With this technique, you won't have to show the property to people who you wouldn't want to do business with anyway. This technique requires you to set certain requirements that potential tenants must meet. Here are some examples:

- The monthly income of the tenant should be at least three times than the monthly rental fees.
- The tenant should be in good standing with all of the landlords he had before.
- The tenant should have a stable job - He must prove that his income is enough to pay the rent.
- The number of people for each bedroom - State laws limit the occupants in bedrooms.
- The tenant must have a good credit history.

Important Note: There are strict laws regarding discrimination. Never discriminate while promoting your property or filtering potential tenants. Avoid the following topics: sex, race, nationality, religion, familial status, skin color, and disability.

Third Step: Show the Rental Property

This is the most frustrating and time-confusing step of the process. That is because tenants are not guaranteed to show up. Here are some techniques that you can use:

- Give them your contact information and the property's address. This way, the tenants can drive by the real estate property first. They can just talk to you if they want to check the interior of the house. Use this technique to eliminate people who don't like the location of the property.

- Divide tenants into batches. Tell them that you will be present in the property for a specific period of time. They can come if they would like to walk through the house. You will have multiple tenants on the property, so it can be awkward. However, it instils an element of scarcity and competition into the mix.

Processing Applications

Allow all of your applicants to fill out the application form, regardless of whether you want them on your property or not. This approach will help you avoid discrimination charges.

Important Note: Ask tenants to complete the application form upon receiving it. Some of them will want to fill out the document later. It would be best if you will discourage this because it prolongs the entire process.

The Application

Rental application forms must require the following pieces of information:

- Name of the applicant
- SSN
- Mobile and telephone number
- The addresses they lived in during the last five years
- Signature of the tenants
- Contact information in case of emergency
- Previous employer (ask for the name of the company, income, hire date, and contact information)
- Current employer (ask for the name of the company, income, hire date, and contact information)

Application Fees

Make sure that each applicant will pay an application fee. Process an application only after receiving this payment.

You may set any amount that you like. Most landlords, however, match their application fee with those of others in their local area.

Important Note: Some states have limitations regarding application fees for rental properties. Check the laws applicable in your area to ensure that you are not doing something illegal. In addition, do not treat this fee as a source of income. Potential tenants will know that you are taking advantage of them.

Disqualifying Applicants

Once a tenant pays the fee, check his application form and search for crucial information before running background checks. This approach can help you streamline the process and avoid wasted time. Here are some things that you must focus on:

- The applicant's employment status
- The applicant's monthly income
- The applicant's housekeeping, property maintenance, and rental payment history
- Number of people in each bedroom

If your tenant earns $2000 each month and your desired monthly payment is $1500, you may remove him from your list. Sometimes, however, undesirable information results from typo errors. That means you need to talk to the applicant first before rejecting him.

Important Note: Explain your criteria for choosing tenants. This way, you can avoid conflict with applicants in case you need to reject them. Do not run credit and/or background checks for people who didn't meet your requirements. You may return their application fee if you want.

Credit and Background Checks

Get more information about applicants who passed your criteria. You can do this by running a credit or background check on the tenants. There are a lot of options that you can use, but landlords often use SmartMove. Basically, SmartMove relies on emails to perform the credit/background check. Just provide the email address of the tenant to SmartMove and wait for the results.

Choosing the right type of credit or background check relies on the market's strength and your location. If your pool of tenants is large, you may implement strict guidelines to find the best tenants. If your potential tenants are few, on the other hand, you may opt for "lighter standards". Some landlords place more emphasis on the income and rental history of the tenant than his credit score.

Credit and background checks turn up various types of information. Here are the ones you must focus on:

- Bankruptcy
- Prior felonies
- Judgments
- Prior evictions
- Other information related to financial or criminal history

Confirming Rental History and Financial Capability

Applicants may give false information, especially when the landlord's requirements are hard to meet. This is the reason why you should confirm everything a tenant wrote on his application. The application form you used should have a clause that lets you investigate the tenant.

Talk to the applicant's current employer. Ask about the former's income, nature of work, and length of stay. Afterward, talk to the applicant's former landlords. The pieces of information you must obtain are:

- The amount of their monthly rents
- The length of their stay in the rental properties
- The landlord's overall impression regarding the tenant
- The tenant's behavior before leaving (e.g. Did he give appropriate notice before vacating the property?)

Accepting or Rejecting Applicants

The results of the credit/background check will help you know your applicants better. At this point, you have a clear idea as to who the best applicants are. There are situations where multiple applicants qualify. Choosing an applicant over another can lead to discrimination charges if the landlord is not careful. You can avoid this problem by processing applications based on the order you received them. This "first-come, first-serve" approach will simplify the screening and selection process.

Don't waste time on unqualified applicants. When denying someone, state the reasons for your decision clearly. Send a written notice to the tenants you will reject. This notice should contain the reasons why the applicant didn't qualify for your rental property.

Inform qualified applicants as soon as possible. Call them or send them a written notice. Keep in mind, however, that the applicant is not guaranteed to rent your property. Potential tenants apply for multiple properties at once. There's a chance that great prospects won't turn into actual tenants.

You can secure great tenants by requiring deposits for the real estate property. This fee is non-refundable. In addition, your tenants must pay it within 48 hours of getting approved. Inform the qualified applicant that other people would like to rent the property, so he must pay the required deposit if he doesn't want to lose his opportunity.

You need to prepare an agreement concerning the deposit. This agreement states the following:

- The deadline of the applicant for signing the lease agreement

- The deal will be canceled if the applicant will not sign the lease agreement by the specified deadline. When this happens, the landlord will keep the deposit.

Important Note: Prepare two copies of the agreement: one for you and one for the tenant. This document will serve as his receipt for the deal.

Preparing the Lease Agreement

Before getting a lease agreement, you must determine the terms that you will use. Do you want a monthly rental setting or an annual lease?

Many landlords opt for one-year leases because it allows them to keep the tenants for a long time. Other landlords, meanwhile, prefer the flexibility offered by a month-to-month lease.

The lease agreement that you need to use depends on the state you are in. You can get this document from an attorney or a local supplier of documents (e.g. Office Depot). If you want, you may go to www.uslegalforms.com or www.ezlandlordforms.com to get the appropriate lease agreement.

States differ in terms of the laws and rules for tenant-landlord transactions. If you downloaded your lease agreement from a website, ask your attorney to review it first. Obviously, you don't want to use an invalid agreement for your rental business.

An effective lease agreement contains the following information:

- The amount of the rent
- The name of the tenant
- The property's address
- The length of the lease term
- Details regarding late fees

- The condition report (see below)
- The amount of the security deposit
- Extra provisions concerning pets, smoking, utilities, etc.

Signing the Lease Agreement

Set a meeting between you and the tenant. It would be best if you'll conduct the meeting in the rental property. If possible, ask the tenant to sign the agreement on the day that they will move in.

You can streamline the signing process by marking the important areas with a highlighter or post-it notes. Once the tenant arrives, discuss all of the provisions of the lease agreement and have them sign on the right parts as you continue.

Collecting the Rent

Get the tenant's first rental payment while he is signing the lease agreement. If the tenant will move in midmonth, don't prorate their initial payment. Rather, prorate the second payment so that it matches the first one. Simply put, your tenant will pay in full for his first month of stay. On the second month, however, his payment will depend on the number of days he stayed at the property during the first month.

The Condition Report

You need to discuss the property's condition before handing the keys over to your new tenant. This phase of the transaction requires a document called move-in condition report. Basically, this report states the property's condition on the day the tenant moved in. Inspect the property together and have him take note of the property's overall condition. Record each problem that you will find. For instance, record the holes and cracks present in the house.

Don't rely on your memory too much while doing business transactions. Put everything on paper. This way, you won't forget about the important aspects of your deal. You will also have a proof that the property was in an excellent condition when the tenant moved in.

Giving them the Keys

Hand the keys over to your tenant once he paid for the fees and signed the required documents (e.g. the lease agreement). If you don't have the tenant's signature and payment, don't allow him to place his things inside your property. Otherwise, you might face nasty consequences.

Inform the tenant about your rules and expectations. If you have specific procedures for rental payments or repair requests, let your tenant know.

Chapter 4: How to Flip Houses

House flipping is a quick and exciting way to build wealth. You'll buy a property, make some improvements, and look for buyers. However, this strategy comes with serious risks. You might lose your hard-earned money if you aren't careful.

In this chapter, you will learn how to flip houses. It will provide you with tips, tricks, and techniques that you can use for your real estate business. Read it carefully - it is a step-by-step guide that will walk you through a complex but profitable process.

Step 1: Commit

This is the first step of any business venture. Many people have the desire to flip houses. They are excited about this strategy - they study it and talk about it. Unfortunately, these individuals don't "cross the line". They are afraid to commit. Keep in mind that flipping houses is a business. It will have a huge impact on your finances. Entering this field half-heartedly is a huge mistake.

House flipping involves complex processes. You need to learn a lot of things in order to succeed. If you are sure that you can spend the time, money and effort to study house flipping, proceed to the next step.

Step 2: Study

Diving into house flipping without the requisite knowledge can lead to financial disasters. This book contains ideas and strategies for real estate investing, so it can serve as a great starting point. However, you also need to obtain more information about house flipping. There are a lot of learning materials out there: you just have to run an online search.

Important Note: Books can't teach you everything. Just like what people say, "experience is the best teacher". Once you have mastered the basics of this investment strategy, go ahead and put your knowledge to the test.

Step 3: Perform a Market Analysis

You should find the market where house flipping is most profitable. In some locations, a $300,000 home is too expensive. In other locations, however, it is considered as too cheap. Markets have different characteristics, so you must understand the market you wish to enter. Answer the following questions:

- How long does it take to complete a transaction?

- What is the average price of available properties?

- What is the price of bank REOs?

- Which area is the fastest in terms of sold homes?

- Which sizes, types and layouts are in demand?

Study your market carefully if you want to survive in it. Visit open houses and talk to local experts. This way, you'll collect important pieces of information that you can use in making decisions.

Step 4: Secure Financing

You can't flip a house if you don't have money. After analyzing and choosing a market, you should figure out how to fund your business activities. You can finance your house flipping business through the following methods:

- Hard Lending - A "hard lender" is a money lender that provides funds for risky ventures (e.g. house flipping) in exchange for high-interest rates and additional fees. A "hard loan" matures within one year, so it is an ideal fund source for house flipping. You can find hard lenders by running a Google search.

- Conventional Financing - You may flip a house using an ordinary bank loan. This method can be difficult, however, especially if the property is in a bad shape.

Important Note: Banks rarely lend money for unfinished houses.

- Cash - This is the best option if you have enough money in the bank. Since you will use your own funds, you won't have to worry about paying interests. However, most "house flippers" don't have this option.

- Private/Partners Funds - Borrow money from someone who has extra cash. This person may want to partner up with you or lend their money. Investors consider it as a cost-effective fund source, although it can be extremely complex.

- Home Equity - Use this option if you have a high equity in your own house. To apply for home equity loans, talk to a credit union or bank near you.

- Mixed - You may also combine the methods given above to obtain the necessary funds.

Important Note: Finalize at least one fund source before looking for a property. If you are planning to use a loan, try to acquire loan commitments. This way, you can immediately buy a great property as soon as you see one. These days, speed is crucial in securing profits.

Step 5: Look for an Agent

Keep in mind that real estate investors don't have to work alone. You can always get the help of other people to streamline your business. In the current process, for instance, you should work with a real estate agent. Don't worry about the costs: you won't pay for anything.

The seller will pay for the agent's services. Why would you miss out on this free and convenient option?

An agent can help you find great properties, prepare offers, compare prices, and other good stuff. Because there are no costs, take advantage of this option completely. Look for an experienced agent who knows how to work with house flippers.

If you don't have an agent, you will likely negotiate with the seller's own agent. The goal of a "selling agent" is to get the highest possible price for his client. Think about it: do you want to work with that type of person directly?

Step 6: Define an Ideal Transaction

Prior to checking real estate properties, you should trim down the possibilities into specific ideas. Your knowledge about house flipping and the market itself can help you with this. Your goal is to flip homes that are easy to sell. Thus, you need to determine which types of properties customers would like to buy. Share this information with your agent. Ask for suggestions and have him email you whenever an interesting real estate property becomes available.

Here are some details that you should provide:

- the location for your flipping activities

- the highest amount that you are willing to pay

- the lowest amount that you are willing to pay

The criteria given above will help you in screening real estate properties. In fact, your quest for a profitable deal can be quick and automatic.

Step 7: Analyze Possible Deals

You can't just purchase the first property that will meet your requirements. Analyzing all of your options is essential in the real estate business. This task is long and complex. But you can simplify it by thinking of house flipping as a game of numbers. Properties differ in terms of their price. Your goal is to find the property that offers the highest potential profit.

There are various online tools that you can take advantage of. For instance, you can boost the speed and accuracy of your analysis using a "flipping calculator". This type of calculator can help you determine the ROI, net profits, and performance estimates of a property. Here's a free and simple calculator: http://www.realmarkits.com/tools/flipping_calculator.php.

You may practice your skills now by visiting online listings of real estate properties. Launch a flipping calculator and run the numbers. Use realistic assumptions for the rehabilitation costs and related expenses.

Step 8: Search

You can use a multiple listings service (also called MLS) to find great properties. But you shouldn't rely on this resource exclusively. Drive around your chosen location and look for potential deals yourself.

In most cases, you'll search for vacant properties or those that require significant repairs. Once you find a property that meets your criteria, contact the owner immediately.

Step 9: Choose a Property

The steps given above will help you find "flippable properties". You might quickly find a great property. However, the search process might also take several months. Instead of worrying about the waiting time, you should concentrate on locating the best property. It is okay to feel excited, but don't let your emotions influence your business decisions. Relax and stay consistent with your chosen criteria.

Step 10: Offer

Send an offer once you find a property to flip. In the real estate industry, you must present the following information to the seller:

- The amount you are willing to pay
- The fund source you are planning to use
- The closing date
- Who will pay for the closing expenses
- Necessary contingencies

It is likely that you need to add more data in your offer. The list given above shows the most important details to include. If you discovered the property with your agent's help, he will help you with the process. That means you won't have to do anything.

If you discovered the property on your own (e.g. through direct mail), your agent won't be able to help you much. Rather, you may fill out a "Purchase Agreement" form. This form is available in office supply stores or local title companies. If you're a total newbie, it would be best if you'll ask an agent or a lawyer to review your document.

Step 11: Work on the Contingencies

In real estate, the term "contingency" refers to an "escape clause" present in an offer. Basically, it is a clause that allows you to cancel a transaction without experiencing financial losses. Contingencies protect your money in case the deal goes sour. But excessive contingencies can discourage the seller from taking your offer.

It would be best if you'll concentrate on the essential contingencies. Here are some examples:

- Financing - You will find this contingency in a non-investment real estate contract. Basically, financing contingency allows the buyer to terminate the transaction in case he can't collect enough funds. If you have a guaranteed fund source, you may waive this contingency.

- Inspection - You cannot determine the actual condition of a property during a "walk-through". No matter how hard you try, you won't see every significant flaw of the property you're interested in. This is the reason why you should get the services of a professional property inspector. With an "inspection contingency", you can cancel a deal in case the inspector finds unacceptable problems.

- Appraisal - This contingency will give you two options in case the appraisal value of the property is lower than the listed price. The first option is that you may cancel the transaction straight away. The second one, meanwhile, allows you to ask for a lower purchase price - you may cancel the deal if the seller will refuse.

Important Note: Contingencies can hurt your chances of getting the property you want. Obviously, sellers wouldn't want to place themselves under strict rules if they can look for other buyers. Because of this, you may want to skip the contingency section of your offer completely. This approach will boost the strength of your offer.

Step 12: Negotiate

You should wait for the seller's response. The response comes in the form of an edited offer (i.e. the seller will modify your offer according to his needs). If you're lucky, the seller might accept your offer and skip the negotiations. Unfortunately, this situation rarely happens.

During a negotiation, you must stay consistent with the targets you specified before. Don't allow your emotions to ruin your plan. For example, don't agree to an undesirable price increase regardless of how "attached" you are to the property in question. Your job is to find deals that you can benefit from. Remember: house flipping is a game that relies on numbers. Focus on the numbers if you want to succeed.

Negotiations end with one of these results:

- Mutual Acceptance - Mutual acceptance occurs when the parties reach an agreement.
- Cancelled Deal - You need to cancel the deal if you and the seller cannot strike an agreement.

Don't assume that you have lost the property after a bad negotiation. There's still a possibility that you and the seller will find a middle ground later on. When the second negotiation happens, buyers typically get a better deal. Stay positive and hope that the seller will change his mind. Meanwhile, search for other properties to flip.

Step 13: Pay

Now that you and the property owner have reached an agreement, you should make a payment called "earnest money". You'll hand this money over to a third-party (e.g. an attorney) to prove that you want to buy the seller's property.

Some investors send the earnest money with their offer. But it would be best if you'll wait for the seller's positive response before sending cash to a third-party. Keep this idea in mind, especially if you are sending multiple offers.

Important Note: The seller won't have access to the earnest money. An attorney or escrow company will keep the money on your behalf.

Step 14: Work with an Attorney or Title/Escrow Company

The documents will go to either an attorney or title/escrow company (depending on your location). Talk to a real estate agent if you have no idea about this. To keep this section simple, let's assume that you will work with an attorney. These third-party entities have the same function so it shouldn't be confusing.

The attorney will help you in closing the deal. He will search for problems (e.g. liens) related to the property and prepare the documents. Once everything is ready, the attorney will set the date for the buyer and the seller to sign the contract.

Important Note: If you have an agent, ask him for an available attorney.

Step 15: Inspect the House

At this point, you should have a property inspector check the house for you. It is tempting to save some money by doing the inspection yourself. However, do not even try the Do-It-Yourself approach unless you know what you are doing. Cutting down your costs at this stage can lead to reduced profits (or even financial losses). A home inspector will give you detailed information regarding the house that you are going to purchase.

If possible, go with the inspector as he inspects the house. Ask questions in order to learn more about house flipping in general. The knowledge that you will gain can help you in your next flipping ventures.

If you are working on a single-family property, the fee for home inspection ranges from $400 to $600.

Important Note: The goal of a property inspector is to search for problems. It's normal to receive a 15-page document containing various issues. In fact, each real estate property has at least 30 things that you need to get fixed. Flawless properties don't exist. Instead of waiting for an imaginary property, look for one that doesn't have serious flaws.

You don't have to fix all the listed problems. Get the inspector's recommendations regarding the issues that must be solved. After receiving the inspector's report, choose one of these options:

- Renegotiate the deal.
- Accept the property's condition and continue the transaction.
- Cancel the transaction.

If there are serious problems with the property, use the first option before relying on the third. Check whether the seller is willing to fix the problems before closing the sale or give you a credit for the repair costs.

Step 16: Create a To-Do List

Create a list of tasks that you should complete to get the property ready for reselling.

Some investors perform this step while negotiating with the seller. This approach is faulty: your work will go to waste if the seller rejects the offer. Additionally, the to-do list is incomplete since a home inspector hasn't checked the property yet. Because of this, create your to-do list once you have secured the deal and received the inspector's report.

An experienced contractor can assist you in preparing the list. With his help, you will determine the tasks that you should complete as well as their corresponding costs. Obviously, you don't want to buy a property whose repair costs are expensive. If you aren't careful, repair costs can turn your house flipping business into a financial nightmare.

Step 17: Look for Contractors

You should find reliable contractors unless you want to work on the property yourself. This task can be complex and challenging. However, you can simplify it by treating house flipping as a real business.

If you don't know any contractor, ask for recommendations from property managers, house flippers, or real estate investors. Request for bids from multiple contractors to make sure that you will get an excellent deal. Investors divide contractors into three categories:

- High-End - These guys work on expensive structures (e.g. malls). They charge thousands of dollars for a paint job since their clients are willing to pay. Use high-end contractors sparingly.
- Average - Average contractors are insured, licensed and bonded. They can be independent workers or employees of small companies. Most average contractors have worked with property managers and house flippers. They charge reasonable fees. This is the best type of contractor for house flipping.
- Low-End - These people have a limited set of tools. You can use their

services without spending much. But remember that they are usually not insured, bonded, or licensed. That means you will have little to no protection in case they mess up. Stay away from low-end contractors as much as you can, except for basic jobs such as lawn mowing.

Ask for written and detailed bids. If a contractor claims that he will paint the interior for $1,500, will he work on the doors too? Detailed bids can prevent potential problems.

Important Note: It is likely that you will work with multiple contractors to finish a project. Specify who will work on what, and when. You also need to indicate the exact amount that you will pay for their work.

Step 18: Finish Your Tasks

You must finish certain tasks while waiting for the contract. Here are some examples:

- Schedule the starting date for the contractors.
- Ensure the property.
- Create a bank account and ask for checks.
- Make sure that utilities and debts have been paid.
- Sign the paperwork that you'll receive from the attorney.

Important Note: Determine the flip's completion date. Because you will run the entire process, you have to make sure that the project will be finished quickly. Prevent "dead days" by planning each phase of the rehabilitation.

Step 19: Complete the Transaction

The real estate property will be under your name now. This is an important milestone in the house flipping process.

Your attorney will specify a time when you can sign the paperwork. Traditional procedures require the buyer and the seller to sit down together during the signing. However, this is completely optional in some areas. The attorney will collect the funds and make sure that the seller received the right amount.

The attorney will have the deed recorded in the county. This process will transfer the ownership of the property to you.

Step 20: Run the Rehabilitation

If you did your best in the 17th and 18th steps, this task will be painless. Your chosen contractor must be prepared to work according to the schedule you made.

You may hire someone to manage the rehabilitation for you. This option comes with costs, however, so you will likely serve as the project manager. Make sure that your contractors will complete their tasks on time and with the expected quality. Contractors tend to exceed the timeframe they initially promised. You need to pressure them so that the project will be completed on time.

Step 21: Take Care of the Finances

Take care of all the bills (e.g. supplies, utilities, contractors, etc.). Monitor and analyze the numbers to make sure that your project stays within the allotted budget. This aspect of house flipping can be confusing and frustrating. Fortunately, you can maintain control over this task by staying organized.

You will work with countless bids, documents, and receipts as you work on the project. Organize all of these and record them in a spreadsheet program. This way, you can take a closer look at your expenses.

Step 22: Check the Contractors' Work

Your contractors completed their tasks. Now, you should inspect the house and go through your to-do list. This approach can help you identify tasks that your contractors forgot about.

Important Note: Notify the contractors regarding each pending task. Do not pay them until they do what they're supposed to do.

Step 23: Stage the House

In real estate, the term "staging" refers to the process of giving a property a "lived-in" feel. It involves the placement of artworks, pieces of furniture, ornaments, and other decorative objects. Staging involves additional costs. But it greatly increases the saleability of your property.

There are staging companies that you can hire. If you're on a tight budget, however, you may contact a local furniture store and have them stage your property.

Step 24: Include the Property on the Multiple Listing Service

The property looks awesome. It's ready for a new buyer (and a high selling price). Now is the perfect time to list it as "for sale". There are a lot of options that you can choose in offering your property in the market. However, most investors choose the Multiple Listing Service (or MLS) route. This option requires you to work with an agent and specify the following:

- The commission of the real estate agent
- The price
- The duration of the listing
- Other pieces of information that your agent will require

Before listing your property, the agent will analyze similar homes nearby that were sold recently. Then, he will decide whether your chosen listing price is appropriate. A high price is nice, but it is useless if it scares potential buyers away. Make sure that the price of the house is competitive.

Step 25: Make Sure that Your Agent Does His Work

At this point, your tasks are limited to three:

• Waiting
• Keeping the property clean
• Answer questions from your agent and potential buyers

You need to rely on your real estate agent, so ensure that he's doing his job. Request for reports and/or talk to him regarding the listed property. This way, the agent will consider your property as a high-priority item.

Important Note: It is likely that your agent is working with many sellers. If you won't exert some "pressure", your property might fall down to the bottom of his list.

Step 26: Receive and Analyze Offers

A buyer sent you an offer. That's good news. However, you cannot celebrate yet. There's a chance that the offer won't become a sale. Counting the profits prematurely won't help you in doing business.

Rather, think of offers as business proposals. Consider their financial implications. Are they profitable? Do they contain a lot of contingencies? Do you think the offers are serious?

Talk to your agent, your adviser, your spouse, and your business partner (if any).

Step 27: Work for a Great Price

It is likely that you won't accept the buyer's initial offer. Rather, you will request for modifications that will benefit you. Buyers expect you to make a "counter-offer", so some back-and-forth discussions are okay.

After negotiating with the buyer, the transaction will either proceed or die out. Hopefully, you and the buyer will find a profitable price point.

Step 28: Let the Buyer Do His Work

Allow your buyer to inspect the property. It's likely that he will hire an inspector to find all of the existing problems.

Your buyer will receive several pages of problems, just like the ones you received while buying the property. The inspector will find many problems, regardless of how well you rehabilitated the property. Be prepared for the buyer's requests regarding repairs and/or price reductions. Analyze his requests well and do everything to close the deal at a profit. If you will be insensitive to the buyer's requests, he might back out from the transaction.

You will work with an attorney to take care of important topics (e.g. loans). Return phone calls and answer emails as soon as you can. This way, you can make sure that there will be no issues coming from your end.

Step 29: Complete the Transaction

Before or during the closing day, you must sign some documents in the office of your attorney. Read the document carefully and look for errors (which often exist). If there's an error, talk to your closing agent immediately.

The lawyer will take care of the payments. He will receive the buyer's payment, settle loans related to the property, and give you a check (or wire the money to your bank account).

Keep in mind that you cannot keep 100% of the money. You need to pay your taxes. Current tax laws consider house flipping as "active income". Thus, the government will tax the transaction at a high level. It's a good thing that you can work with a tax adviser. Prepare a tax plan before closing the deal with your buyer.

Use your profits to fund your next flip. If done properly and consistently, house flipping can help you build wealth in no time.

Chapter 5: Real Estate Wholesaling

More real estate investors are relying on "wholesaling" to build wealth. That's because it doesn't require large funds or extensive knowledge.

In this chapter, you'll know the basics of this profitable investment strategy. Reading this material carefully will arm you with the necessary skills and knowledge.

Wholesaling - The Fundamentals

In real estate, the term "wholesaling" is a process where you will find deals for other investors. You will receive payments in exchange for your services as well as the documents that you will prepare.

For instance, a wholesaler will find people who want to sell their homes. Then, he will look for buyers (e.g. house flippers) who might be interested in acquiring new properties. If the price of a property is $70,000 and the buyer pays $74,000, he can keep the difference (i.e. $4000) as profits. That means you can earn money even without investing your own funds.

Important Note: The example given above relies on a scheme called "assignment". Here, the wholesaler assigns the property to the buyer. There are other wholesaling schemes that you can use. You'll learn more about these schemes later on.

Is this Strategy Legal?

Wholesaling is not 100% legal. In some situations, local authorities might consider it as a violation of state or federal laws. That means you need to familiarize yourself with the laws and regulations applicable in your area. Talk to an attorney before pursuing this real estate strategy.

Brokering

Wholesaling can be illegal because it involves "brokering". Basically, "brokers" are people who assist in completing business transactions. A broker must have a license before he can look for potential deals. Unfortunately, there is no specific license for real estate wholesalers. Working without a required license is against the law.

How to Wholesale Real Estate Properties Correctly

If you don't want to get incarcerated because of real estate wholesaling, do the following:

- Acquire a broker's license - This approach is self-explanatory. If you have a license, you can act as a broker without fear of the law. You have to shell out some cash, but you will be able to sleep at night peacefully.
- Purchase the property before selling it - You will learn more about this scheme later. Instead of "assigning" a property to someone, you will purchase it yourself (even for a short time only) and resell it to someone else. Real estate experts refer to this strategy as "double closing".

Important Note: The tips inside this section are not guaranteed to prevent law-related penalties. Keep in mind that states and countries have different laws. It would be best if you'll talk to your attorney before wholesaling any property.

Does it Require Down Payments?

Just like what you saw from the previous example, you can wholesale a real estate property without spending money. But that is an overly simplified example. It assumed that you already have a seller and a buyer who are willing to give you a profitable deal.

Remember this: buyers and sellers won't come to you automatically. You need to do various things to find deals that are profitable for all the parties involved (including you).

Wholesaling demands marketing skills. In fact, you need to be a great marketer if you want to succeed in your wholesaling business. As you probably know, marketing often involves expenses.

The Problems that Wholesalers Face

Wholesaling promises quick and easy profits. You just have to arrange deals for interested parties. Unfortunately, this strategy is not for everyone.

To become a successful wholesaler, you should have:

- Great communication skills
- An eye for profitable deals
- The ability to estimate the post-repair value of a real estate property
- The ability to estimate the rehabilitation expenses
- Negotiation skills
- The ability to estimate rental fees

- Knowledge about financial calculations for house flipping
- Knowledge about financial calculations for rental properties
- Excellent marketing skills
- The ability to persuade people even in difficult situations

As the list above shows, wholesaling requires different types of skills and abilities. You may outsource some tasks, but you must understand how each aspect of your business works.

In addition, you will compete with people who can purchase properties without wholesale fees. For instance, a buyer might find the seller on his own efforts. That means you and the buyer will compete for a single property. You want to sell the property at a higher price in order to get some profits. The buyer, on the other hand, can pay the current price. In this scenario, it is likely that the seller will choose to work with the buyer directly.

Important Note: The details you've read are somewhat scary. Well, don't be scared. Many people have built wealth using this real estate strategy.

This part of the book aims to reveal the truth regarding wholesaling. Its goal is to educate you and prepare you for what's waiting out there.

How to Find Excellent Deals

Wholesalers need to find excellent deals. If you don't have a deal, you won't earn any money. That means you need to establish a system for locating deals. Let's use the word "system" because you surely want to wholesale more than one property. With a reliable system, you can wholesale real estate properties one after another.

In most cases, you must spend considerable time and effort on each deal. It's important to fill your system with various leads. The process of converting a lead into a completed deal involves searching for sellers, conducting inspections, calculating expenses, finding potential buyers, preparing bids, and having the agreement signed. It's likely that you will work on 10 different transactions simultaneously. As a wholesaler, your ultimate goal is to turn all of your leads into profits.

This part of the book will focus on obtaining leads. Real estate wholesalers use a wide range of methods in finding buyers and sellers. The most popular methods are:

Drive

You may drive around certain places to find great deals. Search for "distressed" properties. Often, a distressed property has boarded up doors/windows, unkempt lawn, legal notices, and other signs of neglect or issues.

Multiple Listing Service

The "Multiple Listing Service" is the set of deals available in the real estate market. Many agents and investors are using this method to locate possible transactions. You will experience fierce competition but you will likely find some deals you can benefit from. Wholesaling a foreclosed property is difficult but lucrative.

Important Note: With this method, you may work with an agent to wholesale a deal.

Direct Mail

The term "direct mail" refers to the process of sending mails to potential sellers. Real estate sellers buy lists of names from www.mellisadata.com and www.listsource.com. Send letters to the property owners and encourage them to contact you back.

Calculate

Math is a complicated subject. It can make your head swirl, but it is necessary. Don't dabble with real estate wholesaling if you don't understand the calculations it requires.

One good thing about real estate mathematics is that it's only difficult during your first few tries. Once you get used to this type of math, you'll just breeze through several pages of computations. Additionally, there are many tools that you can use (e.g. online calculators). For now, let's focus on the fundamentals of "wholesale mathematics".

Determining the Right Price

Your goal is to find a great transaction for others. Thus, you can identify the best price point by "working backwards". Remember that the goals of your buyer have a huge impact on the potential sale. For instance, if you are selling properties to house flippers, these people must benefit from any potential transaction or you won't get business from them.

Real estate experts use the term "Maximum Allowable Offer" (or MAO) when referring to the said price point. Basically, MAO is the highest price that you can offer to the seller in order to get your desired profits. You can get this data using the After Repair Value (or ARV). ARV refers to the selling price of the property once the rehabilitation process is completed. Deduct the relevant expenses from the ARV in order to get the MAO. The costs that you should consider are:

• The profit you want to make
• The fixed costs (e.g. holding costs)
• The rehabilitation costs
• The profit the flipper intends to make

Here's the formula:

Maximum Allowable Offer = After Repair Value - (Fixed Costs + Repair Costs + Wholesaler's Profits + Flipper's Profits)

Understanding the Numbers

You probably noticed that wholesale math relies heavily on your estimates. For example, you need to estimate the fixed costs, repair costs, and post-repair value of the property. Experienced wholesalers can give reliable (if not accurate) estimates. Newbies, however, may hire a coach or do some research. The former involves large expenses, so choose the latter. You can streamline this task by using a wholesaling calculator.

A wholesaling calculator is an online tool that can quickly determine the MAO of a potential transaction. You can get the information you need by entering some numbers and answering several questions. Run an online search to find available wholesaling calculators.

Getting the ARV

Wholesaling calculators are great. But they have a glaring limitation - they cannot identify the property's after repair value. The ARV serves as the starting point of the entire calculation process. Thus, you should get an accurate ARV before calculating anything.

Real estate experts utilize various methods in finding the ARV. But you can distill these methods into a basic principle: the after repair value of a property is almost equal to that of similar properties nearby.

It's almost impossible for you to find a property that is identical to the one you're working on. Well, an exact match is not necessary. You can just look for a property that share some similarities with your target and make some corrections. For example, if the property you are selling has four bedrooms and the closest basis you can get has three bedrooms, adjust the numbers to reflect the differences.

Important Note: The quickest and simplest way to get the ARV is by working with an agent. Real estate agents can easily find comparable properties. They also possess extensive knowledge when it comes to estimating values. However, this option involves costs. Most agents are too busy to render services for free.

Make an Offer

Make an offer right after identifying the MAO. During this phase, you will put your negotiation skills to the test. Sign the contract once the negotiations come to a close. The type of contract that you need to use depends on the state you live in. Some states allow the use of standard sale and purchase documents. Other states, meanwhile, let you buy agreements from online stores or paper supply companies.

You have several methods to choose from when closing the deal. The contents of your contract largely depend on your desired closing strategy (e.g. double closing).

With the "assignment" scheme, write "and/or assigns" to the right-side of your name (i.e. in the area for the name of the buyer). This phrase means you and/or another person you choose will purchase the real estate property. Foreclosed homes are usually not compatible with this scheme, but most sellers don't fret about it. Transparency is an essential element of wholesaling. Make sure that the seller knows what you are trying to do.

In the "double closing" scheme, you may sign the contract under your own name or that of your business. "Double closing" is an investment scheme where you will buy a property and resell it to someone else quickly. If you lack the funds, you may borrow money from lenders. These people will give you the cash and ask for a repayment within 24 hours.

Look for Cash Buyers

If the deal is full of potential, you may keep it for yourself. Flip it or rent it out. If you want to stick with your wholesaling activities, however, you need to sell the deal as soon as you can. This way, you can look for more leads and profitable deals.

According to real estate experts, wholesalers have to find cash buyers. Basically, cash buyers are people who can purchase a property in cash. The money doesn't have to belong to the buyers themselves. It doesn't matter whether the money came from the buyer's bank or from a lender. The important point here is that the buyer won't apply for a loan. He can surely buy the house.

Often, a cash buyer is a house flipper or a rental property investor. Flippers and landlords are always on the lookout for great deals. They have the cash for such transactions.

These days, wholesalers are joining expensive programs just to find cash buyers. But a "premium list" of cash buyers isn't necessary. You can find these buyers almost everywhere. You just have to be creative and resourceful in your own search. For example, you may place ads in the local newspaper or work with real estate agents. Look for people who bought properties that are similar to the one you are selling.

Important Note: In general, a cash buyer is looking for a deal himself. All you need to do is prove that you can help him in earning more profits.

Receive the Payment

This is the last phase of the process. Now that you finished all the hard tasks, you just have to collect the payment.

You don't have to do anything difficult. Just forward the important documents (e.g. assignment contract) to a lawyer or title company and wait for them to do their job. It would be best if you will look for attorneys or title companies that have previous experience with wholesalers. You may talk to the wholesalers in your area and ask about their preferred attorneys/title companies.

Once everything is done, the buyer will acquire an awesome real estate property. The seller will get the payment. You will receive your share of the profits.

That is your money so you can spend it any way you want. You may purchase a car, a cellphone, a laptop, etc. If you want to succeed in the world of real estate, however, invest your fresh profits back into your wholesaling business. Use the funds for marketing or similar activities. This way, you will close other deals and earn more money.

Chapter 6: How to Lease Out a Real Estate Property

Many real estate investors lease out their properties to generate income. With this strategy, you can hold on to a property and milk it for continuous financial gains.

This chapter will discuss the important aspects of leasing. It will describe the fundamental ideas related to leasing a real estate property. It will also teach you how to include leasing in your investing "toolbox".

Leasing - The Basics

Leases are contracts that describe the conditions under which a person (or a group of people) will rent another person's real estate property. They guarantee that the tenant (also known as the lessee) will be able to use the asset in question. In addition, leases make sure that the landlord (also known as the lessor or property owner) will receive payments from the tenant within a specific period of time. Any party who will violate the contract will face consequences.

Keep in mind that each lease is a binding contract. It is a legal agreement that specifies the terms and conditions of renting a real estate property. If you want to rent out your apartment, for instance, you should prepare a lease that defines the amount of monthly payments, the due date of each payment, the consequences of missed payments, the security deposit you will require, the maximum number of occupants, whether the tenant/s can keep pets, and similar pieces of information.

Require the lessee to sign the contract. Signing the document means he agrees to the conditions you stipulated.

The Consequences of Breaking Leases

The consequences for breaking a lease can be mild or grave. The situation under which the violation was made has a huge effect on the severity of the penalty. For example, if your tenant will break the lease without negotiating with you, he might face a lawsuit, a negative mark on his credit history, or both.

With this kind of violation, the tenant will also experience difficulties in finding another rental place to live in. Lessees who must break leases multiple times usually seek the help of a lawyer or make arrangements with their respective landlords.

If a tenant will break his lease, you will be able to keep his security deposit and/or get another tenant (hopefully a better one). Because of this, you might actually allow your tenants to break their leases.

Important Note: There are leases that allow early termination through special clauses. Basically, an "early termination clause" helps your tenant in ending the agreement if you (i.e. the landlord) will not fulfill the obligations you agreed upon. For example, if you won't fulfill the repairs you promised in the lease, your tenant may opt for an early termination.

The Different Parts of a Lease Agreement

Because leases are legally binding, they should contain correct pieces of information. They should also cover important elements of the contract such as property possession, rental payments, duration of the contract, etc. In this part of the book, you'll discover the most important parts of lease agreements:

Possession

This part discusses the tenant's right to possess the rental property. As the landlord, you should allow the tenant to utilize the property for lawful purposes and activities. In addition, you must not interfere with how the tenant will use your property.

Important Note: You will always have the right to visit the rental property. This principle comes up in the repairs-related part of the agreement.

Duration of the Contract

An effective lease has specific starting and ending dates. If your lease agreement indicates its termination date, you won't have to instruct the tenant to leave. He should vacate the property according to the recorded date of termination (unless you formed a new agreement with him).

A lease can last for months, years, or even decades. In some states, the duration of a lease cannot exceed 100 years. Some states, however, allow this curious arrangement.

Often, a lease agreement defines the overall time period, the starting date, and the termination date. For example, your lease will run for three years: from October 1, 2016 to September 30, 2019.

How the Lessee can Utilize the Rental Property

You can divide leases into different categories (e.g. retail, residential, office, etc.). Each category comes with natural limitations on how the tenant can use the property. For example, if you are renting out a residential property, the tenant cannot use it as a home office. If your lease is for retail purposes, however, you may specify the types of merchandise that the tenant can sell in your property.

Property Maintenance

The maintenance-related aspects of a lease vary based on the property's nature (i.e. whether it is commercial or residential). When it comes to residential properties, the landlord must take care of all the repairs and/or maintenance. For commercial properties, however, the lease may contain various clauses that hold the tenant responsible for some (if not all) of the maintenance costs. Make sure that your lease agreement clearly defines the obligations of both parties.

For office or retail spaces, the tenant may be responsible for the repair and maintenance of fixtures (e.g. cabinets). The landlord, on the other hand, will take care of the building maintenance.

Security Deposit

In most cases, leases require the tenant to make at least one security deposit. This deposit protects the landlord from potential property damages or missed payments. States have strict policies regarding the handling of deposits. In fact, some states require the landlord to pay interest to the tenant based on the latter's amount of deposit.

You will return the deposit to a tenant once the lease agreement expires. However, you need to make sure that there are no damages in your property before handing the money over.

The Tenant's Options

The tenant usually has the option to renew his lease before its end date. After notifying the landlord, the tenant may renew the contract - the term of which is defined in the lease agreement.

Subleasing and Property Assignment

In real estate, "subleasing" means re-leasing a property to someone else. The original tenant retains some of his interests. In property assignment, however, the original tenant will transfer all of the leasehold rights to the second tenant.

Lease agreements can specify whether subleasing and property assignments are allowed. The agreements may also describe the conditions under which the said maneuvers can be done. Usually, the original tenant will still be responsible for his rental payments and any damage to the landlord's property.

Property Improvements

In general, the landlord doesn't have to make any improvement in the leased property unless stated in the contract. If the tenant wants to request for property improvements, he must prepare a written agreement and ask the landlord to sign. As an alternative, the tenant himself may pay for the property improvements. However, the tenant should talk to the landlord first - the latter will be the sole owner of the improvements the former will make.

Commercial leases usually contain improvement clauses. Retail and office spaces often require changes - changes that fall under the "improvements" category. The tenant needs the said changes in order to run his business.

The Mistakes that You Should Avoid

Leasing your real estate property is not easy. If you want to maximize your earnings from your rental property, you need to avoid the errors that inexperienced landlords commit. This part of the book will discuss the twelve mistakes you must avoid. The mistakes are:

- Leasing out the best spaces immediately - Leased properties are not created equal - some are better than others. If you will fill the greatest spots of your property too soon, the overall value of the remaining areas will fall. That means you need to balance the areas that you will lease out. Fill the not-so-good areas with tenants whenever you can.

- Setting an incorrect price for the property - Setting a high price for your properties is understandable. Higher price means more income.

However, exaggerated pricing can scare away potential tenants. Keep in mind that high-priced properties are useless if they have no tenants. Find a competitive and profitable amount to attract and retain lessees.

- Getting tenants without an overall plan - Leased properties can help you build wealth. However, since leasing involves contracts and long time periods, it is not compatible with the hit-and-miss approach. You need to create a strategic plan for your leasing activities. Then, stick to that plan as you search for tenants and maintain your property.

- Hiring real estate brokers without criteria - Brokers differ in terms of the properties they specialize in. It would be best if you'll find a broker that specializes in leasing properties that are similar to yours. This way, you can be sure that you are working with people who understand your business.

- Using bad termination clauses - If the termination clause of your lease agreement is faulty, the tenant will have an easy time vacating the property. When that happens, you will lose money in the form of unamortized expenses.

- Ignoring "tenant compatibility" - You can't just sign tenants who will come your way. Make sure that all of your tenants will have a harmonious relationship with each other. For example, setting a plain dental clinic beside a popular retail store can lead to conflicts.

- Positioning the property as similar to other properties - It is likely that you are facing fierce competition. There are so many properties to choose from and insufficient number of tenants to fill them all. If you want to attract great tenants, you should differentiate your property from that of your competitors.

Create a compelling idea, message, or story that you can directly link to your real estate property. You may also create a theme for your property if you want. Most real estate investors don't even think about differentiating their properties. Even a basic story can help you attract more tenants and earn more money.

- Spending money on unimportant things - Improving the property is necessary in order to attract tenants. However, you can't just spend your capital on stuff that won't enhance the attractiveness of your property. Before shelling out your cash on improvements, determine whether the said improvements will help in enhancing the property's value and overall quality.

- Ignoring the effects of lease agreements on your overall investment goals - Consider your long-term investment strategy when leasing your properties. Each business activity that you'll make regarding your real estate portfolio should be compatible with the ultimate goals you created. If you'll forget about this simple rule, you will likely face strategic problems in the future.

- Failing to keep the property in good shape - Most tenants are sensitive to the "small things" that landlords ignore. Make sure that vacant spaces have open blinds and working lights. You should also keep the common areas clean and in excellent condition.

- Failing to check the finances of the tenant - This is a fatal error if you are leasing out a commercial property. Before signing the tenant, investigate his finances, revenue stream, and overall business plan. It is also important to ask for a security deposit.

- Failing to assess the competitors - You are not the only player in your local real estate industry. Thus, you need to consider your competitors when formulating plans for your leasing business. Compare your property with those of your competitors in order to find your pros, cons, unique advantages, and areas of improvement.

Chapter 7: Financial Analysis for Real Estate Investors

Financial analysis is an important part of any real estate transaction. It can help you determine whether you can profit from a deal. If you don't have this skill, you will have poor chances of making profits. You might even risk your hard-earned money in bad transactions.

In this chapter, you'll learn how to analyze potential transactions. You will discover the basics of financial analysis and how you can use it for your real estate business.

Financial Analysis - The Fundamentals

Financial analysis is the process of checking the financial aspects of a property, transaction, or business proposal. As a real estate investor, you will use financial analysis to know the profit (or loss) that you'll gain from a property. To keep this chapter short, it will focus on multi-unit residential properties. However, the ideas you'll find here also apply to other types of real estate investments.

With a single-family property (either personal or investment), you need to consider the "comps" (i.e. comparables) present in the market. Basically, a comparable is a nearby property that has the same properties as the one you are working on. That means a property will experience "appreciation" if similar properties in the local area are increasing in value. If the comps are depreciating, the property in question will depreciate as well.

Larger properties (i.e. properties with two or more units) involve a different pricing method. In this kind of property, you won't have to look at comparable properties in the market. You just have to determine the income-generation capabilities of the property to know its market value. This idea is evident in rental properties. It's not surprising to find large rental properties appreciate while other real estate properties dwindle in value.

How to Collect Data

You must understand the different elements of property value in order to make an accurate financial analysis. For real estate experts, financial analysis is the process of converting various pieces of data into one or more financial models. Those models, on the other hand, should produce data that shows the profitability of the investment.

Here are some of the most important pieces of data for reliable financial analyses:

- Income - It refers to the income-generation capabilities of the property.
- Expenses - It refers to the maintenance costs required by the property.
- Purchase Details - It refers to the costs that you'll incur when purchasing the property. The rehabilitation costs, improvement expenses, and purchase price belong to this category.
- Property Information - It refers to the physical aspects of the real estate property (e.g. square footage).

Actual Data and Pro-Forma Data

The income potential of a multi-unit property dictates its value. The more profitable the property is, the higher its market value. This is the main reason why sellers tend to give slightly exaggerated numbers. They claim that they receive high income from their properties or exclude some expenses. Through these techniques, they make real estate properties more appealing.

To prevent the issues outlined above, you need to gain access to fresh and reliable market information. This data will help you in completing an effective financial analysis. Most real estate investors rely on estimated (also known as "pro forma") data from the property owner.

They use this information to begin the analysis. However, the results of the analysis are only good for filtering deals. You can't rely on them since they came from the seller's personal estimates. Before buying the property, ask for the actual records (e.g. tax bills).

You are lucky if the actual records match the pro forma data. Unfortunately, it doesn't happen often. The seller intends to profit from the transaction, so it is normal for him to use his "creativity".

Important Note: In some cases, the actual and pro forma records aren't enough. You also need to get additional information regarding the property. This way, you can uncover nasty surprises that might turn your dream deal into a financial nightmare.

Data Sources

Here are the best sources of information:

- Income - You can get this from the seller. As mentioned earlier, don't rely on the seller's estimates.
- Expenses - Just like income, the expense-related data will come from the seller himself. You can verify the information with the help of a professional building inspector. This person can identify potential repairs and their corresponding costs.
- Financing Information - Identify the down payment your seller requires. Also, talk to a mortgage broker or money lender to know the loan-related expenses.
- Property Information - You can get this data from the seller.
- Purchase Information - The seller will give you his desired purchase price. It's likely that you can negotiate with the seller if his initial price is too high. Keep in mind, however, that you will pay for

rehabilitation once the transaction is completed. That means low-priced properties are not guaranteed to be profitable.

Financial Analysis in Action

In this section, you will apply the ideas given above to a fictitious property. This example will show you how to perform financial analysis on real estate properties.

Let's say you have talked to the seller, the lender, and the closing attorney. Here are the pieces of information you obtained:

- Interest Rate - 5% (30 years, fixed)
- Finance Amount - 75% of the costs
- Listed Price - $500,000
- Improvements - $20,000
- Closing Costs - 1% of the costs
- Down Payment - 20% of the price

The tables given below add more details into the mix:

Cost-Related Assumptions	
Price	$500,000
Down Payment	$100,000
Improvements	$20,000
Closing Costs	$5,000
Total Costs	**$625,000**
Cash Outlay	**$125,000**

Finance-Related Assumptions	
Down Payment	20%
Finance Amount	$400,000
Down Payment Amount	$100,000
Interest Rate	5.0%
Mortgage	30
Amount of Each Mortgage payment	$2,147.29

These assumptions will help you in completing the computations below:

How to Get the Net Operating Income

The Net Operating Income (also known as "NOI") is an important metric of every financial analysis. Basically, NOI refers to the revenue the real estate property generates minus the costs. Most investors compute NOI using the monthly expense and income information of the property. Multiply the resulting value by 12 in order to get the annual data.

To get the NOI, you should:

- Evaluate the income of the property - The term "gross income" refers to all of the revenue that a property generates. For this example, let's assume that the property has 10 units that earn $500 each per month. Additionally, the property's laundry facilities generate $250 each month ($3,000 per year). Based on these numbers, the property's gross monthly income is $5,750.

- Important Note: You can't assume that all of the units are occupied. By considering unit vacancy, you will come up with reliable calculations.

Here's another table:

		Per Month	Per Year
Income			
Rent		5,000	60,000
Vacancy Rate	10.0%	(500)	(5,000)
Net Income from Rents		4,500	54,000
Other Revenue		250	3,000
GROSS INCOME		**4,750**	**57,000**

- Evaluate the costs - Here are the costs that you need to deduct from the gross income:

- Insurance
- Advertising
- Utilities (if applicable)
- Management (if you have a property manager)
- Maintenance
- Property Taxes

To keep things simple, let's assume that the annual expenses of the property are $13,150.

- You can get the NOI of the property by deducting the annual expenses from the annual revenues. In this example, the formula is:

- *Revenue - Expense = NOI* or *$57,000 - $13,150 = $43,850*

The Performance Metrics of Real Estate Investments

At this point, you have the data needed to decide whether the property is a good investment or not. The first part of this chapter listed several outputs. To keep this material short, let's focus on the Rates of Return and the Cash Flow. There are many only online tutorials regarding the calculation of other financial metrics.

The Cash Flow

You probably noticed that the preceding calculation didn't mention the debt service. That is because the NOI specifies the property's income level regardless of the property owner's mode of financing. The annual or debt service payment is directly related to the financing model of the owner (i.e. the interest rate, amortization schedule, down payment, etc.), which means it will render the NOI useful only for the financing plan being used.

Buyers differ in terms of their financing models, so you should have a financial metric that focuses on the real estate property (instead of the buyer).

This is the reason why you need to calculate the cash flow of the property. Basically, the cash flow is the NOI less the expenses for debt services (e.g. the payments). Keep in mind that "cash flow" refers to the profits you'll get from the property by the time the year ends. This amount will decrease if you will make a lot of payments for debt services. The NOI and the cash flow will be equal if you purchased the property in cash.

The monthly mortgage payment for the property is $2,147.29. Thus, your annual payments for debt services is $25,767.48 (i.e. monthly payments * 12). Calculate the cash flow using the formula given below:

NOI - Debt Service Payments for the Year = Cash Flow / $43,850 - $25,767.48 = $18,082.52

Important Note: You've learned that buying a property in cash maximizes your cash flow. That means it is the best way to finance your real estate investments, right? Not necessarily. This is because there are other factors to consider aside from the cash flow. For example, you need to consider the ROI (see below) of the property before adding the latter to your real estate portfolio.

Return on Investment

For most real estate investors, the ROI is more important than the cash flow. In essence, the ROI is the amount you will receive in relation to your initial investment. To get this metric, you need to use the following formula:

Cash Flow / Initial Investment = Return on Investment

You will get a high ROI if at least one of these conditions is true:

- The cash flow is high
- The initial investment is low

Real estate properties differ in terms of their ROI. To determine the reasonable ROI for the property you're working on, analyze the following aspects:

- The Cap (or Capitalization) Rate - This aspect of the ROI doesn't have any direct relationship with the buyer or his financing model. Calculating this value is easy - you just have to divide the NOI by the price of the property (i.e. *NOI / Price = Cap Rate*). Real estate experts claim that if you can only analyze on ROI element, focus on the cap rate.

In the current example, the property's cap rate is: *$43,850 / $500,000 = 8.77%.*

- Important Note: In general, a cap rate of 8% to 12% is great. However, you should also consider the cap rate of comparable properties in your area. For example, if similar properties have an average cap rate of 12%, a cap rate of 9% is not that attractive.

- The "CoC" (or Cash-on-Cash Return) is the actual return rate you'll get from your invested cash. To get this metric, you need to divide the property's cash flow by your investment. In this example, the CoC is: *$18,082.52 / $100,000 = 18.08%* (i.e. *Cash Flow / Initial Investment = CoC*).

- The Total Return on Investment - There are other factors that influence the financial performance of a property. These factors are:

- Property Appreciation - This factor is difficult to predict. But you should try to get a reliable estimate since it affects your future financial gains.
- Accrued Equity - Your tenants will pay off the property on your behalf.
- Tax Consequences - You can earn or lose funds because of taxes.

- The main difference between the Total ROI and the CoC is that the former considers the aspects that influence your profits. The latter, on the other hand, focuses on the relationship between your return and the property's cash flow. Use the following formula when calculating the total ROI:

Total Returns / Initial Investment = Total ROI

- In this formula, "Total Returns" consists of different elements (i.e.

appreciation, taxes, cash flow, and equity accrual). We need to make some assumptions to calculate the total ROI of the imaginary property:

- Property Appreciation = $9,500
- Equity Accrual = $3,300
  - Tax Effects = $0 (To retain the simplicity of this example, let's assume that taxes have no effect on it.)

  - The property's total return for the current year is: *$18,082.52 + $9,500 + $3,300 + $0 = $30,882.52*. Thus, its total ROI is: *$30,882.52 / $100,000 = 30.88%*.

Chapter 8: How to Build Your Own Real Estate Portfolio

Like other forms of business, real estate investing requires techniques and detailed strategies. You can't just purchase properties like a madman and hope that profits will come in droves. Investing involves risks, and your job as an investor is to minimize the risks and maximize your returns. If you want to become a successful real estate investor, you need to formulate strategies and utilize certain techniques.

In this chapter, you'll learn about different techniques and strategies that real estate investors use. The ideas that you'll get from this chapter came from the arsenal of investing gurus such as Robert Kiyosaki.

How to Formulate a Strategy

Basically, a strategy is a systematic course of action that you create to attain a specific goal. Creating an effective plan involves seven steps:

First Step: Identify Your Ultimate Goals

You don't have a strategy if you don't know what your goals are. This step requires creativity and imagination. What would you do once your real estate business succeeds? Will you spend more time with the people you love? Or will you travel to the world's most exotic places? You may also dream about owning a house in different countries.

Aggressiveness is okay. These dreams are close to you: they aren't targets that your financial adviser imposed on you. Some people dream about attaining complete financial freedom in ten years. That target is achievable, especially if you have a great strategy in place. By determining your ultimate goals, you will have a clear idea about the things you need to do.

Second Step: Determine Your Financial Objectives

Now, you should focus on the financial aspect of your ultimate goals. Specify the amount of money that you need as well as the deadline for reaching your goals. Next, list down the value of your assets and deduct your liabilities. The number that you will get is known as "net worth".

Third Step: Set Targets for Your Cash Flow

At this point, you must determine the amount of money needed in attaining your ideal cash flow. The following formula can help you with this task:

(ideal cash flow) x 20 = target

If you want to have $250,000 as your annual cash flow, for instance, you must earn $5 million.

Fourth Step: Evaluate Your Current Financial Status

You have completed the goal-related tasks of your strategy. It is time to assess your current status in terms of assets and liabilities. Focus on the assets that you can invest immediately (e.g. cash). Don't include your cars or golden necklaces. You may include your home equity if you can invest through a loan. Divide the assets into two groups: liquid and non-liquid. Here's an example:

Liquid Assets

- Bonds
- Stocks
- Savings
- Mutual Funds
- Certificates of Deposits
- Other

Non-Liquid Assets

- Business
- Gas
- Oil
- Receivables
- Intellectual
- Real Estate
- Other

Fifth Step: Set Your Values, Vision, and Mission

Now that you know your goals and current financial status, it's time to form the first parts of your plan. Your plan must have your values, your vision, your mission, the real estate properties you'll focus on, and the factors that you'll consider in selecting properties.

You're probably doubts about the relevance of values and vision/mission statements in becoming a real estate investor. Well, these elements are extremely important if you're planning to become a successful (and wealthy) investor. Owning real estate properties is like owning a real business. That means you need to set your values, vision, and mission while forming your "business plan".

Your vision is a statement that concentrates on the future. Your mission states what you will do in managing your investments. Values, meanwhile, are the exact values that you'll follow as an investor.

Sixth Step: Choose a Niche

Investing in a wide range of properties can be confusing. It would be best if you'll focus on a particular niche. This way, you can invest your time, money, and effort in becoming an expert investor in your chosen niche. For example, you may concentrate on commercial or industrial properties. The type of property that you will choose should match your personal preferences and ultimate goals.

Seventh Step: Identifying the Selection Criteria

This is the last part of your strategy. Specifying the criteria for potential investments is crucial. Unfortunately, most investors ignore it. Incorporating your criteria into your strategy can prevent stress, headaches, and wasted effort. It can also prevent expensive blunders. If you will do this step properly, choosing the best real estate properties will be a walk in the park.

Here's an example:

Criteria

- Rate-of-Return - 40%
- Appreciation - 8%
- Price - $250,000 to $500,000
- Time Commitment - 10 hours each month
- Price-to-Value Ratio - 8.5 : 10
- Required Amount - $100,000
- Cash Flow - Neutral or Positive

Building Your Team

You don't have to manage your business alone. Like other businessmen, you should find skilled and experienced people to work with. These individuals will increase your leverage: they will give you their time, contacts, resources, talents, and knowledge. Instead of trying to learn and do everything, you can request for help from your team.

How to Build a Team

The following tips will help you find excellent members for your team:

- Create a Plan - Identify the skills and resources you need. For instance, your team should have a banker, a lawyer, an accountant, a property manager, etc. Once you know the skills you need, finding the right people will be quick and easy.

- Look for Referrals - In most cases, you'll find great team members through referrals from friends and family members. However, you should focus on referrals from other real estate investors. You may also get referrals from an accountant, lawyer, or financial advisor.
- Secure Agreements - Set clear agreements with every member of your team. Specify what you need from them and what you can offer.

Accounting

Business owners understand the importance of accounting. Great accounting results to great reporting. Great reporting, on the other hand, results to great decisions. You won't be able to decide properly if you don't have access to crucial pieces of information. If you will ignore accounting, you won't know whether your investments are generating your desired profits. To incorporate great accounting into your real estate business, you should:

Perform Accounting With a Clear Goal in Mind

Don't perform accounting just to avoid issues with the IRS. The main purpose of accounting is to generate useful and precise data for business-related decisions. Uninformed investors assume that accounting is only useful for preparing tax returns.

Focus on Accuracy

Great accounting is more than just bookkeeping. The former starts with correct bookkeeping entries. With the right bookkeeping techniques, you can generate useful financial reports.

Bookkeeping is a process in which you will record transactions for analysis and reports. Most real estate investors outsource bookkeeping tasks to accountants. If you want to do it yourself, however, you may use accounting computer programs like QuickBooks.

When working on your bookkeeping tasks, you should consider the following:

- Chart of Accounts - This "chart" is the group of accounts that you will use to classify receipts and expenses. Use accounts that you understand clearly. For instance, you may place "printer paper" under "Office Expenses" or "Office

Supplies". It depends on your preferences. Keep in mind, however, that you must set an account for everything you want to report.

- Data Entry - After listing the accounts, you should start recording the information. Make sure that each transaction has details.

- Journal Entries - The QuickBooks program automatically sets the credit and debit for each receipt or expense. However, you should make manual corrections if there are no cash transactions. You will do this using your journal entry. Preparing journal entries is easy: you just need to enter the debit and the credit of an entry.

Update Your Books

According to experienced investors, you should work on your books at least once per week. Failing to do that leads to two serious problems. First, you won't be able to make proper decisions and accurate reports since your financial data is outdated. Second, your tasks will pile up and become overwhelming. You will likely put it off as much as you can. By working on your books weekly, you can keep your records manageable and relevant.

Be Consistent

Identify the right accounts and utilize them for similar expenses and receipts. Putting paper costs under the office supplies category is okay. But you should not put it under another category afterward. Consistency is a crucial element of great accounting.

Reports

Successful investors use metrics to manage their portfolios. Simply put, metrics is the measurement of an investment's daily results. You may use raw numbers (e.g. cash flows) or metrics as metrics. Some entrepreneurs compare the current result with previous ones. With this approach, they determine whether or not their strategies are working.

Important Note: Understand the numbers if you want to understand your business.

Let's discuss each type of report in detail:

Cash Flow Statement

Investors consider cash flow statements as the best source of raw financial data. Unfortunately, most real estate investors don't have a clear idea about their actual cash flow. You must understand the flow of cash in your entire real estate portfolio and the flow of cash from all the properties you own.

Many investors assume that analyzing cash flow statements is as simple as looking at the "beginning" and "end" sections of the respective documents. If you are planning to build wealth through real estate, you need to go beyond this superficial "analysis". The best way to use a cash flow statement is by checking the sources and destinations of your cash.

It all starts with your operating income. The operating income consists of rents less typical cash expenses (e.g. maintenance, repair costs, management fees, etc.). Then it shows non-operating entries such as investing and financing transactions.

An investing transaction is a transaction in which money enters or exits your business. It results from investing activities such as a down payment for a newly acquired property or rent from your tenants. A financing transaction, on the other hand, involves money that enters or exits your portfolio because of borrowed money. A mortgage payment is an excellent example for this category.

After listing and computing the said values, you will see whether your cash increased or decreased. It would be best if you will analyze three periods: monthly, quarterly, and yearly. You can use this data to know the status of your cash flow (i.e. either negative or positive) and how your business operations affect it.

Ratio Analysis

Here are some of the financial ratios that you can use:

- Return on Investment - This ratio tells you the total returns that you can get from your properties. The formula that you should use is: *(income + change in the property's value) / initial investment*
- Current Ratio - With this ratio, you can determine your capability to settle liabilities. To get this data, you must divide your current assets by your current liabilities.

- Debt Coverage - This ratio shows whether or not you can pay debts using your cash flow. Use the following formula:
  net operating income / debt service
- Cap Rate - It tells you the revenue that you can get from your real estate properties. Here, you need to divide your net operating income by the value of your property.
- Cash-on-Cash Return - This ratio indicates the cash return from your investments. The formula for this is:
  (cash from investments - taxes) / initial investment
- Debt/Equity Ratio - This ratio shows your leverage. To get this information, you must divide your overall debt by your net equity.
- Loan-to-Value Ratio - Like the debt/equity ratio, it indicates the investor's leverage. You can get it using the following formula:
  debt / the value of the property

Important Note: Real estate investors usually focus on ROI and Cap Rate.

Comparisons

This is the third type of reporting that you can use. In this approach, you'll compare the actual result of your business with other information (e.g. previous performance, expected results, industry standards, etc.). Let's assume that you expected a new property to experience an annual value appreciation of 5%. By the end of the year, however, the value of that property increased by 10%.

Aside from the current appreciation, your report must indicate the average property appreciation for that period as well as your expected rate of appreciation. With these numbers, you will know how your investment performs compared to your expectations and the market itself. If the numbers are great, you might want to purchase similar properties. If you are not satisfied with the numbers, however, you might sell the property and acquire a better one.

Taxes

You should consider tax laws if you are dreaming about immediate profits from your properties. In this part of the book, you'll learn the tax-related aspects of your business.

Important Note: According to real estate investors, you can maximize a property's ROI by taking advantage of existing tax laws. Most of these laws benefit real estate investments. In many countries (e.g. the U.S.), tax laws favor investments that are related to real estate.

The techniques outlined below will help you in maximizing the tax benefits from your properties. These techniques are designed for investors in the U.S., but they also work in other countries since tax laws tend to be similar. Study these techniques carefully: they can help you get more than 30% reduction in your income taxes.

First Technique: Create a Tax Strategy

Aside from your investment strategy, you also need a strategy for your taxes. Basically, tax strategies aim to reduce or eliminate income taxes permanently.

When formulating your tax strategy, you need to consider all of your assets. Think about the stocks, bonds, or businesses that you own. You should also analyze things for the long-term.

Important Note: This task requires the help of a skilled tax strategist. That means you must have a tax consultant in your investment team.

Second Technique: Choose the Right Business Structure

Using the right business structure is crucial. Should you opt for a partnership, a corporation, or an LLC (i.e. limited liability company)? Or is it best if you won't use a separate entity? Some countries don't require separate entities for businesses. In the U.S., however, choosing the right structure can help in preventing lawsuits.

When it comes to asset protection, an LLC is likely your best option. In addition, LLCs offer excellent flexibility. They can "behave" as a partnership, a corporation, or a sole-proprietorship.

If you own rental properties, go for a partnership or sole-proprietorship structure. Listing rental properties under a corporation is a huge mistake. If you will set up your business as a corporation, you will experience financial disasters whenever you take out a property from the corporation.

Real estate dealers and developers should choose to establish a corporation. This strategy also applies to people who "flip" houses. With a "corporate structure", you can minimize the resulting social security taxes. You won't face horrible tax consequences since property distribution only happens during a sale.

Third Technique: Utilize Your Expenses

Most countries, including the U.S., tax a business based on its net income. That means you can reduce your income tax by increasing your deductible expenses. Some real estate investors overlook the tax deductions from meals, travel, and entertainment costs. In the U.S., you can deduct the expenses of meals and/or entertainment if you incurred the costs in relation to an important business discussion.

For instance, this principle applies to sporting events you watch with a business partner. It's likely that your spouse is also one of your business partners. If you will watch the NBA Finals with your spouse, you will also discuss your business. Because of that "business discussion", you can list down the entertainment costs as deductible expenses for your income tax.

To deduct travel expenses, you must prove that you traveled because of your real estate investments. Basically, you need to show that you worked on your business for at least 50% of every eight-hour business day. It covers meetings with buyers or real estate agents.

Fourth Technique: Take Advantage of Depreciation

In the world of real estate investing, depreciation is a gift from above. Typical assets such as machinery suffer from depreciation - their lifespan and usefulness decrease as time goes by. However, land areas do not lose their value (unless a market-related anomaly is happening). In fact, the value of a real estate property increases continuously over the long-term.

Current tax laws allow you to deduct depreciation from your income tax. With real estate, you will deduct depreciation for something that enjoys appreciation (i.e. an increase in value).

Fifth Technique: Document Your Transactions Properly

Make sure that you will document your expenses, earnings, and deductions properly. If your documentation is bad, the IRS might negate your deductions and increase your income taxes. The main element of proper documentation is detailed accounting.

There are various types of documentations that you need to keep. For meals, travel, and entertainment, store all the receipts and take note of the related information (e.g. your companions, the place you went to, the topic of your discussion, etc.). For deductions related to vehicles, you must separate the "personal miles" from "business miles" you have driven.

Proper documentations are boring and time-consuming. However, they are crucial if you want to enjoy a lot of tax deductions. You can take the sting out of this task by working on your documents at least once a week. This approach will help you manage your records easily. If you can't determine the things to record, talk to your tax adviser.

Important Note: The IRS will doubt your listed tax deductions if the latter don't have proper documentations.

The Garbage In, Garbage Out Principle

You will base your investment decisions on projected financial information. When you are dealing with numbers, the quality of your output is the same as that of your input. If you are making decisions based on faulty assumptions, you can't expect your investments to be profitable.

It is true that real estate investing is more than just a number-crunching activity. However, numbers play a huge role in the survival (let alone success) of your real estate portfolio. When conducting a research, focus on reliable and relevant records (e.g. historical information from comparable areas).

You can make decisions based on pro forma data. But these decisions are nothing but intelligent guesswork. If you want to make correct decisions, try to get actual data or at least modify pro forma information so that it becomes more relevant to your situation. For example, make some adjustments on the pro forma records so that they show numbers that match the overall market expectations.

If you can make reliable sales and cost projections, you will have an easy time estimating profitability and cash flow numbers. If you conducted your research properly, you can prevent the "garbage in, garbage out" disease that has corrupted countless asset portfolios. Analyze the historical data of your desired property as well as that of similar properties in nearby areas. Ignoring this basic rule can lead to huge financial losses.

If you are lucky, your faulty decisions can generate thousands (or even millions) of dollars. But why would you rely on luck if you can make reliable projections and business decisions? Building wealth with real estate properties is easier if you will rely on actual data. Eliminate the guesswork from your business analysis. You'll be glad that you did.

Chapter 9: Refinancing a Real Estate Property

This chapter will focus on loan refinancing. It will explain the what, when, and how of refinancing for real estate properties. Read this material carefully: it will help you keep profitable properties in your investment portfolio.

Refinancing - The Fundamentals

The term "refinancing" refers to the act of replacing loans with new ones. In general, the new loans should be better than the old loans (e.g. in terms of interest rate, payment flexibility, etc.). With the refinance option, you will pay off the current loan and transfer the balance to the replacement loan.

In the world of real estate, "refinancing" means replacing existing property loans with better ones.

Here are the main reasons why you will choose to refinance:

- To reduce the fees
- To reduce the interest rate
- To get a flexible repayment model
- To take care of other liabilities
- To utilize your home equity
- To consolidate loans
- To do business with a new money lender

Additional Information

Refinancing has a lot of similarities with applications for new loans. The process it involves is almost identical to the one you went through during the initial loan application. For instance, you need to prove your ability to repay the loan by showing different documents (e.g. bank statements, pay slips, tax returns, etc.).

Most real estate investors think that refinancing is a complex task. However, you can get the help of professionals. Banks usually offer specialists who can help you with your refinancing applications.

The Questions that You Must Answer

Refinancing is not for everyone. Don't assume that because others have used it successfully, you can benefit from it too. There are a lot of things to consider. Here are some examples:

- Your desired repayment flexibility
- The amount of time in which you'll keep the property in your real estate portfolio
- The repayment period

Important Note: You can get the repayment period using this formula:

expenses incurred because of your new loan / annual savings you can get from your new loan = payback period

How to Get a Lower Interest Rate

Countless homeowners and real estate investors have enjoyed the interest-related benefits of refinancing. These people talked to different money lenders and searched for the best loan term and interest rates. In addition, you may lower the interest of your loan by getting a shorter repayment period, removing the insurance requirements of your lender, or making additional mortgage payments.

The "How" and "When" of Refinancing

It doesn't matter how long you have owned your home - you should try to refinance your loan when interest rates for mortgages decrease. In this part of the book, you'll learn how to include refinancing in your investment arsenal.

The Things You Need to Know

Refinancing can be difficult, even for people who owned real estate properties for decades. Your payment history and the increase in your income cannot guarantee an approval for your refinancing applications. That is because refinancing requires you to apply for another loan.

Regardless of whether you are working with a new lender or not, you must submit documentations for your assets, your income, your credit rating, your work history, etc. You should qualify for your desired loan. However, you also need to consider the property in question: its appraised value must be enough to back the new loan.

Additionally, refinancing involves costs. The expenses vary based on the applicant's location but they average two to three percent of the loan. "Cost-free" refinancing loans exist, but they involve high-interest rates and/or large loan balances.

Important Note: If your goal for refinancing is to reduce your payments, calculate the length of time needed in recouping the resulting costs. For instance, if the cost of your refinanced loan is $2000, and you are saving $150 each month, you will start saving money after 13 months. This is an important detail for homeowners and real estate investors.

Refinancing and Your Wealth-Building Strategy

Consider your overall wealth-building strategy when deciding whether to apply for refinancing or not. For example, if you want to reduce your monthly payments and the interest rate, you may refinance your loan when the general interest rates go down. If you have a high equity on your property, you may get some cash from it using a refinanced loan. You can use the resulting funds to take care of home repairs, property improvements, or high-interest liabilities.

As an alternative, you may apply for refinancing to shorten the duration of your loan (e.g. from thirty years to twenty years). That means refinancing can help you pay off the loan quickly. Keep in mind, however, that shorter repayment periods involve higher monthly payments (even if the new loan has lower interest rates).

Refinancing and Your Investments

Refinancing is an excellent choice if you want to keep the real estate property for a long time. That is because refinancing involves costs - selling the property without recouping the refinancing-related expenses is a horrible thing.

It would be great if you will talk to a money lender regarding refinancing and your investment strategy. If you are dealing with an experienced and knowledgeable lender, you will learn many things regarding the pros and cons of refinanced loans for real estate investors.

Chapter 10: Addendums and Amendments in Real Estate Contracts

In this chapter, you'll learn the basics of amendments and addenda. This material will focus on how the said topics affect real estate contracts.

Addenda

An addendum is a distinct section of the buyer's initial offer. If the seller accepts the offer, the addendum will become an "agreed-upon condition".

Let's assume that you are buying a new property. You are a dentist and you want to set up a home office in that property. When you submitted the initial offer, you are not sure whether local policies allow the establishment of a home office. Here, it's necessary to place an addendum on your contract. That addendum should state that you will only purchase the property if establishing a home office is legal.

The contents of real estate contracts differ by location. If local laws allow the usage of addenda, however, you can use the latter to define and demand agreement on aspects that are not related to the real estate contract itself.

For example, you may use an addendum to demand a complete property survey. You may also include addenda in your contract that require inspection and disclosure forms.

Amendments

An amendment is a change that you want to implement on a contract. It is something you want to include in the contract even if you and the other party have made an agreement.

For example, you discovered that a neighbor's fence encroach the property. You would like to get that structure moved before closing the deal. If you want to make your request official, you should "amend" the contract. Keep in mind that you have agreed to, and signed on, the contract by the time you made the additional request. This is the reason why an amendment is necessary.

It's normal for buyers and/or sellers to request amendments to signed contracts. These requests may result from newly discovered issues, property appraisal concerns, title-related problems, etc.

Let's assume that you are buying a real estate property. The most recent appraisal of the property gives lower numbers than the ones you agreed upon. This situation requires significant changes in the contract (and the negotiation itself). You will surely want to get a lower price. The seller, on the other hand, will likely keep a high price in order to secure profits. You and the seller can find a mutually-beneficial change to the original agreement. In that case, amending the contract is necessary.

Chapter 11: 1031 Exchanges

Owning a real estate property gives you access to a wide range of benefits. In particular, rental properties can help you reduce your taxes. Aside from property depreciation (which gives you nice tax deductions), you can use 1031 exchanges to make the most out of your real estate activities (e.g. selling a rental property).

Remember that 1031 exchanges involve various rules and policies. For example, you need to complete each exchange properly if you want to enjoy the resulting tax benefits. In this chapter, you'll learn how 1031 exchanges work when it comes to rental properties. Because taxes have a huge effect on your "bottomline", you need to read this material carefully.

Important Note: It would be best if you'll talk to a lawyer or an accountant to clarify tax-related questions.

1031 Exchanges - The Fundamentals

1031 exchanges are transactions that involve two similar real estate properties. One of the properties is sold while the other one is bought. The transaction will occur within a specific period of time. The IRS implements various limitations regarding this type of transaction. However, there are no clear definitions of the said limitations. The basic requirements of 1031 exchanges are:

- Both parties should be the owner their respective properties for at least one year before the transaction
- The transaction must be conducted for business-related purposes
- The parties must specify the replacement real estate property within 45 days. They should also buy the property within 180 days.

If you will satisfy these requirements, you can sell a property without paying taxes on the recaptured depreciation or profits.

The Taxes that 1031 Exchanges Cover

You must pay taxes for the profits you'll earn from any real estate property you will sell. In addition, you must pay the recaptured depreciation (for rental properties). You can enjoy depreciation-related deductions for your rental properties because the IRS assumes that your property has a limited useful life and that its value decreases each year.

Landlords consider depreciation as a great add-on to being an owner of a rental property. Unfortunately, you need to pay the tax deductions if you will sell your rental property at a price that is higher than its depreciated value.

Analyze the following example:

- You bought the property for $200,000. The market value of its structure is $180,000.
- If you will hold the property for more than ten years, the total income tax deductions that you can get is about $64,000.
- Selling the property for $200,000 will result in a tax liability of $64,000. The latter amount will appear as income tax.

If you have been holding your property for a long time, your recaptured depreciation amount can be staggering. Fortunately, you can use a 1031 exchange to avoid taxes.

Important Note: The estimated depreciation of most rental properties is based on a 27.5-year schedule. A rental property will depreciate completely after 27.5 years. Thanks to 1031 exchanges, you may sell depreciated rental properties without any taxes. Then, you may purchase new properties with fresh depreciation schedules.

1031 Exchanges and House Flipping

The IRS implements strict guidelines for house flippers who want to use 1031 exchanges. Obviously, the IRS won't allow a house flipper to use the 1031 exchange "route" in avoiding taxes. To execute a 1031 exchange for a house flip, you must meet the following requirements:

- You must rent out the repaired property for at least 1 year before selling it.
- Do not list the property for sale until you have completed the "1-year rent out" condition.

How to Complete 1031 Exchanges

You need the help of a third-party in order to complete a 1031 exchange. There is no specific list of people who can act as the intermediary. However, the following individuals are prohibited:

- The accountant of the taxpayer
- The attorney of the taxpayer
- The real estate agent of the taxpayer
- Any person who works for the taxpayer
- Any family member of the taxpayer
- Any business partner of the taxpayer

The third-party will keep the money after the first real estate property is bought. He will use the funds to purchase the replacement property. As the owner, you should declare the property you want to exchange before selling it. After the transaction, you must find another real estate property and tag it as the replacement. The declaration of the replacement property should occur within 45 days of the sale. Then, you will have 180 days to purchase the replacement property.

How Funds are Handled in 1031 Exchanges

During a 1031 exchange, you must use all of the money from the transaction to acquire a new property. If you won't, you will pay taxes. Additionally, the price of the replacement property should be at least equal to that of the old one. The IRS will require you to pay income taxes if your new property is cheaper than your previous one. In general, you will pay taxes based on your unused funds or the difference between the properties' selling prices.

You are probably wondering why you must purchase a real estate property that has the same price as the previous one. The reason for this is simple: liabilities. If your house is on a $200,000 loan, selling it for $400,000 and purchasing a new one worth $200,000, you will still earn some profits. You utilized 100% of the funds from the transaction, but you used some of it to pay off your debt. The IRS considers the paid debt as a form of financial gain.

Title-Related Concerns

The name that you'll use for the title of the replacement property should be identical to the one listed on the original property's title. Keep in mind that you can't sell the property to anyone who is related to you.

Reverse 1031 Exchanges

In a "reverse exchange", you will purchase the replacement property before selling the current one. Obviously, this option is not for everyone - you must use other fund sources to finance your purchase.

Real estate investors use this option because buying another property within 180 days can be difficult. By preparing the replacement property, you can secure the benefits of a 1031 exchange without worrying about any deadline. This is an essential strategy for large businesses that exchange expensive and complicated facilities.

Refinancing and 1031 Exchanges

You can use refinancing to get some funds out of a 1031 exchange. For example, your cash from the exchange is equal to $200,000. Then, you used that money to acquire the replacement property. Locking up that amount of money is wasteful. Refinance replacement property after acquiring it, and you won't have to pay taxes for the funds you will receive. For the IRS, funds from refinanced loans are not profits.

1031 Exchanges and Personal Residential Properties

At the time of writing, you can use a 1031 exchange to acquire personal residential properties. This strategy protects you from taxes. Exchange the real estate property with one that you like to move into in the future. Rent out the replacement property for at least one year. Then, move into that property and stay there for two years.

You may live in the property as long as you want. If you will stay there for two or more years, you can sell the real estate property without paying any taxes. This strategy involves certain requirements so discuss it with your lawyer or accountant first.

Chapter 12: How to Analyze Risks

Risks have a huge effect on the profitability of any business venture. As a real estate investor, you should know how to identify and evaluate risks. If you know how to perform risk analysis, you'll have better chances of avoiding faulty investment decisions.

In this part of the book, you'll discover how risk analysis works in real estate investments. You will learn its fundamental concepts and step-by-step procedure.

Risk Analysis - The Basics

Before making any investment decision, you need to understand the risks present in your situation. Then, determine the effect and possibility of all the risks you discovered. The goal of risk analysis is to find the factors that can influence your investments.

The Different Methods of Risk Analysis

Real estate investors divide risk analysis methods into three categories:

Quantitative

A quantitative method allows you to set values for the risk levels of a business decision. The most popular quantitative methods are:

- Computer simulation
- Evaluation of effects
- Evaluation of likelihood

Qualitative

- Investors and businessmen rely on qualitative methods when making business decisions. Here, the person will analyze risks based on his intuition, experience, knowledge, and judgment.
- This is the method you will rely on if numerical information is not available.
- Qualitative methods allow you to make quick decisions. However, it is not ideal for time-sensitive or resource-intensive situations.

Here are the most popular qualitative methods today:

- Delphi Technique
- Assessment of multidisciplinary groups
- Structure Interviews
- Brainstorming
- Survey

Semi-Quantitative

Semi-quantitative methods require you to classify risks using descriptive words (e.g. low, high, medium, etc.) or detailed descriptions. An appropriate measurement tool (e.g. a scale) should accompany the said classifications. If you are not careful with your descriptions or measurements, misinterpretations will occur.

The Monte Carlo Method

This is a quantitative method that you can use in analyzing risks. With this method, you will use a mathematical model to represent the reality. Assigning different numbers to the model generates different results and situations.

This method requires a lot of iterations (i.e. you need to assign values randomly). That means you will have a large sample size to be used as the basis for your analysis. You can produce the iterations using an information processing program.

After obtaining a sufficient number of iterations, you need to perform a statistical analysis. This analysis will help you in formulating conclusions regarding the existing risks.

Risk Models

A risk model allows you to apply the Monte Carlo method in your analysis. A risk model represents the reality using a set of mathematical computations. You should calculate the major risks and compare them with other variables present in your current situation. You also need to analyze the risks with regards to economic variables.

How to Create Your Own Risk Model

- Identify the risks that might affect your investment.
- Discover the behavior of the risks (i.e. know the variation range of each risk).
- Find out the likelihood of each risk. Here are the distribution functions that you can use for this task:

- Discrete - Here, you will choose the values you want to consider. You also need to associate a likelihood value to each risk.
  - Triangular - This distribution function has predetermined maximum and minimum values. The risk with the most likelihood is known, and the function appears as a tall pyramid.
  - Uniform - Just like the triangular function, a uniform

function has predetermined maximum and minimum values. The risks between the maximum and minimum values have equal chances of occurring.

- Determine the function that is appropriate for the existing risks.
- Assign a value to each function and run a simulation.
- Choose the variables that you'll use as the basis of your analysis. Most real estate investors choose "Net Profit" and "Net Present Value" for this process.
- Run a simulation program to get the right number of iterations. There are a lot of simulation programs available online. You can run a Google search to find the one that suits your hardware.
- Collect the results of the simulation and use them as the basis for your conclusions.

Chapter 13: How to Manage Risks

You will spend considerable time, money, and effort in establishing a real estate portfolio. Unfortunately, consistent revenue streams cannot guarantee eternal profits. You must protect your assets to make sure that your labor won't go to waste. Creating a risk management strategy can help you in securing the success of your real estate business.

In this chapter, you will learn the basics of risk management for real estate properties. This material will discuss the basics of risk management as well as the step-by-step process of managing risks.

How to Minimize the Risks

Some individuals purchase real estate properties without understanding the risks they will be exposed to. It is true that being a real estate investor can help you build wealth quickly. However, it comes with serious risks - you can get bankrupt or incarcerated if you will ignore or underestimate the risks.

According to recent reports, real estate owners (landlords, in particular) face more lawsuits than any other kind of businessmen. Thus, you should do everything you can to protect yourself from legal, personal, and financial risks that will come up. Here are some things that you can do to prevent lawsuits:

- Inspect your real estate properties on a regular basis - Treat property inspections of your maintenance programs seriously. Obviously, the simplest way to reduce chances of lawsuits is to check your real estate property and solve detected problems. Keep the results of your property inspections. These documents will prove that you addressed problems promptly and properly.

- Address the complaints of your tenants - Respond to people who are voicing their concerns regarding your real estate business. If you can build a reputation of being a responsive owner, you will have excellent protection against negligence-related lawsuits.

- Eliminate existing risks and prevent new ones from appearing - This is one of the best ways to prevent lawsuits. Here, you'll just remove things that introduce risks to your real estate business. For instance, you may remove the pool slides, diving boards, and similar structures from your residential properties.

- Assign the risks to other people - You can transfer risks to someone else by purchasing insurance and/or hiring suppliers and contractors. Ask for a written proof that the supplier/contractor covers the property in question. This documentation is a crucial requirement before accepting materials or services.

Important Note: The methods given above can help you minimize risks. However, they cannot remove all of the risks present in real estate investing. That is the main reason why you need to get insurance for your real estate properties. These days, insurance plays an important role in maintaining a profitable asset portfolio.

How to Get the Right Insurance

Real estate investors consider insurance policies as one of the greatest protections against property damages and financial losses. In fact, insurance coverage is a crucial element of effective risk management plans.

There are a lot of insurance agents out there. These people are smart and convincing - they will tell you that their insurance products can cover and protect you from any unfortunate event that can happen to your property. However, since insurance products come in different types and prices, you cannot just rely on the words of a stranger.

You must see through his flowery words, identify the creative embellishments, do your own research, and choose the right insurance coverage for your real estate investments. The insurance product that you'll choose must offer great coverage and affordable pricing.

Important Note: Make sure that the coverage you are paying for is appropriate for your property. Insurance policies can be of great help. But they are next to useless if they protect you from something that won't likely happen.

Lawsuits are common these days. That means you need to get an insurance product that covers you and your real estate properties. Keep in mind that insurance policies are not limited to actual damages to your property. You can also use an insurance to protect yourself from claims and other legal concerns. Facing a lawsuit in itself is not that troublesome, especially if you know that you didn't do anything wrong. It's the costs of keeping a good lawyer that troubles most investors.

More Information Regarding Insurance Products

Insurance products can guard you against financial losses resulting from various events (e.g. storms). Top-tier insurance policies, however, also protect you from liabilities (e.g. losses or physical injuries experienced by other people because of your property). Additionally, liability protection covers the expenses related to injury lawsuits.

The Usual Coverage of Insurance Policies

Here are the three main types of coverage offered by insurance companies:

- Basic - This is the most affordable coverage out there. Despite its name, a basic insurance policy protects you from losses caused by fire, smoke, riot, vandalism, explosion, lightning, windstorm, vehicles, aircraft, earthquake, and volcanic eruptions.

A basic insurance policy doesn't cover certain items (e.g. machinery) unless indicated specifically in the insurance endorsement. You may enhance the coverage of a basic policy by purchasing add-ons (e.g. protection from falling objects.

- Broad-form - With this type of coverage, you'll get all of the benefits offered by basic packages. You will also enjoy protection from damages resulting from water damage, weight of ice/snow, glass breakage, structural collapse, and falling objects.

- Special - This type of insurance protects you from everything, except the ones specified in the policy itself. It is the best form of insurance product that you can get. However, it is also the most expensive.

Payments from insurance companies come in two forms:

- Replacement Expense - Here, the insurance company will reimburse the replacement costs. The physical depreciation of the property doesn't matter. You need to pay more money in order to enjoy this coverage. But treat this insurance as an important investment.

- Actual Value - The insurance provider will reimburse the replacement costs. However, the amount will decrease based on the property's physical depreciation. This is the most popular type of reimbursement that insurance companies use.

Important Note: The age, type, quality, and location of your property determine your "insurance premium" (i.e. the payments you need to make for the insurance coverage). Because insurance premiums can be extremely high, you should get a quote from an insurance company before purchasing a property. This way, you can make sure that there are no premium-related surprises related to the new property.

The Renter's Insurance

Your tenant needs to pay for a distinct insurance program called "renter's insurance". Basically, this insurance protects the tenant from losses caused by theft, water damage, fire, or other unfortunate events. With this insurance, you can enjoy additional protection without additional costs.

Insurance Claims

If an incident happens within your property, record the facts and share them with your insurance company as soon as possible. This is an important rule, especially if the incident involves physical injuries. It is true that your insurance policy has clear definitions regarding the covered incidents as well as the appropriate reimbursement amounts. However, the insurance company won't hand the money over to you without a "fight".

There will be an investigation first. Because the condition of the property plays a crucial role in such investigations, you should take photos of the incident if you can. If you have photos as evidence, you will have higher chances of getting the reimbursements.

Insurance companies usually have a deadline for filing claims (e.g. 30 days after the incident occurred). Thus, file a claim as soon as you are able.

Chapter 14: How to Raise Capital

Many people want to own real estate properties. They know the benefits offered by this kind of asset. They are more than willing to invest. The problem is that they don't have the funds. In the world of real estate, you need money to earn money. You should make a huge investment if you want to build wealth through real estate properties.

In this chapter, you will discover the tricks and strategies that investors use in raising capital. After reading this material, you will have a complete arsenal of fund sources.

The Required Amount

When buying a property, a real estate investor often pays the down payment from his own pocket. Then, he will borrow money to pay for at least 50% of the property's total price. This is the most popular funding method among investors today. It is popular for a reason: it can help you earn a lot of money even without a large upfront capital.

Most lenders require a borrower to pay at least 20% of the property's price before processing a loan application. Some lenders offer great loan terms to borrowers who pay at least 25% to 30% of the purchase price. Keep in mind that lenders require higher down payments when the value of real estate properties falls.

When it comes to residential properties (e.g. single-family houses), paying 20% to 30% of the total price as down payment will give you excellent financing terms. It is likely that you can make a lower down payment (e.g. 10%). However, the loan fees and interest rates associated with your mortgage will be high.

How to Obtain Funds through Your Savings

You should know how to save money if you want to build wealth. By saving your income (regardless of the source), you will have excellent opportunities to expand your investment portfolio. Countless investors have used this strategy in their real estate strategies. These people saved their money and purchased properties one after another.

Here are two things that you can do to save more money:

- Decrease your expenses - This is one of the quickest and simplest ways to save money. Live beneath your means in order to generate positive cash flow. This process starts with analyzing your expenses. How much do you spend for food, clothing, transportation, and other stuff? Once you have recorded the information, choose the expenditures that you can reduce. For instance, if you spend thousands of dollars on your out-of-the-country vacations, try to decrease the number of your trips. If you really love to travel, however, look for places that won't hurt your finances much.

- Look for other sources of income - You can increase your net income by getting another job or finding a job that offers a better salary. Regardless of your preferred option, you must spend time on the things that are important to you. For instance, don't sacrifice your health, sanity, and personal relationships just to earn more funds.

- You should also invest in your own education. Upgrading your knowledge will help you earn more from your current profession and succeed in the real estate world. For instance, you may study the art/science of property management and/or property appraisal.

How to Take Care of Down Payments

New investors usually lack funds for their first property acquisitions. Don't worry if your capital doesn't meet the 20% down payment requirement - purchasing a property is still possible. You may switch to another investment approach (which gives you better control over your finances), or seek for outside funding. Let's discuss these options in detail:

Using a Different Approach

If you don't want to borrow cash from other people, you may try the following techniques:

- Look for low down payment loans - Some lenders will approve your loan even if your down payment is just 10% or less. However, they require loan applicants to buy PMI (i.e. private mortgage insurance) for the loan. The PMI, which costs hundreds of dollars each year, protects the money lender in case the borrower defaults on the loan. Keep in mind that PMI is not mandatory if you will make a 20% down payment.

- Focus on small and/or cheap properties - If you don't have much capital, don't look at expensive properties for now. Rather, search for properties that are within your budget. Small real estate properties and those that require some repairs are your best bet. You may also buy a duplex, rent out a unit, and live in the remaining one.

- Delay the purchase - Buying properties without sufficient funds comes with undesirable loan terms and additional fees. You can avoid these problems by delaying the purchase. Try to save money first. Once you have enough capital, go ahead and buy the property.

- Find low-entry cost options - You can use a REIT (real estate investment trust) to keep your entry costs low. You can buy this asset from a stock broker. In general, a REIT costs thousands of dollars. If you have a retirement account, however, you can buy it for less than $1000.

Obtain Cash from Outside Sources

Real estate investors rely on the following fund sources:

- Home Equity - You may loan money against your equity on your personal property. In general, personal properties are better than investment properties when it comes to interest rates and loan terms. The lender will face lower risks, which allows them to reduce their required interest rates. Because the interest rates are low, you will have more funds to spend or reinvest in your business. In contrast, rental properties pose high risks to money lenders. That means you'll face high rates when borrowing money against your rental properties.

- Important Note: Refinance your first loan if the current interest rates are low. This way, you can free up equity without taking a credit line or home equity loan.

- Retirement Savings - Some companies allow their employees to borrow money against the latter's retirement balance. This option requires the borrower to return the funds within a certain period of time (usually measured in years). There are requirements that you must meet in order to be eligible for this fund source. If you are a first-time homebuyer, you can borrow about $10,000 from an IRA account.

- Transfer Capital from Other Assets - Once you have gained considerable knowledge and experience in real estate investing, you may transfer the funds from other assets such as bonds and stocks. As discussed in an earlier chapter, real estate properties are better than most assets available to you. Focusing on real estate investments comes with risks, however. Consider the following:

- Tax Concerns - Long-term income tax rates apply to investments that you hold for one year and above. At the time of writing, the maximum rate for such revenues is only 15%. You can even get a 0% long-term tax rate based on the income tax bracket you belong to. Thus, avoid selling assets that you haven't held for at least one year.

- Diversification - Don't put all of your eggs in one basket. Basically, diversification means investing your funds in different types of assets in order to spread the associated risks. For example, if you will purchase stocks and real estate properties, you will have good chances of earning money even if one of these assets falls in value.

How to Utilize Advanced Funding Schemes

Complex funding schemes can help you improve the profitability of your real estate portfolio. In this part of the book, you'll know how to apply these schemes in acquiring new properties.

Leverage Existing Properties

If you purchased the right properties and managed them correctly, the overall value of your portfolio will increase. You can use that profit to purchase more properties without worrying about taxes. Real estate investors refer to this strategy as "hypothecation". Here, you will borrow money against your equity on an existing property.

Buy a property and wait for it to "appreciate" in value. Then, tap the resulting equity to borrow money and purchase another property. Repeat this process until you establish a large real estate portfolio.

Important Note: As a businessman, you shouldn't overextend yourself. Analyze the market and look for potential problems. The main drawback of borrowing money against appreciating properties is that it relies on the condition of the market. If the market for real estate properties collapse, you might lose some (if not all) of your properties. In the worst case scenario, you can even become bankrupt.

Look for Business Partners

This is an excellent scheme if you're not contented with small, low-value properties. For instance, you may purchase a real estate property with one or more partners. Business partners offer three distinct advantages: (1) diversification, (2) risk reduction, and (3) additional capital. If you have partners, you can distribute the risks among yourselves and obtain a large pool of funds for property acquisition.

Important Note: Partners can also provide you with complementary skills and knowledge. When searching for potential business partners, focus on people whose goals, experience, and knowledge complement yours.

Take Advantage of Seller Financing

Some sellers are willing to help their buyers with regards to financing. In fact, there are real estate owners and developers who allow less than 10% down payments. Investors treat seller financing as a valuable resource, especially when they have limited capital. You may set these deals as installment transactions. This method allows the seller to reduce his tax liabilities by extending the income report.

The main problem with seller financing is that your options are severely limited. Few seller-financed properties are available, and these are still unsold for various reasons. You will discover these problems during the inspection or after purchasing the property.

Important Note: Stay away from "distressed" properties (i.e. properties with serious problems), regardless of the seller financing that comes with it. Keep in mind that acquiring a property is just the first step of a long and complex process. Often, an affordable property is useless if it requires costly repairs.

Conclusion

Thank you again for purchasing this book!

I hope this book was able to help you to create a stable and profitable real estate portfolio.

The next step is to expand your portfolio by purchasing more properties. Lease out your properties to other people or flip houses. There is a wide range of real estate strategies you can choose from. Analyze each potential deal before risking your hard-earned funds. If you have studied this book correctly, you'll have excellent chances of earning millions of dollars through your portfolio.

Finally, if you enjoyed this book, please take the time to share your thoughts and post a review on Amazon. It'd be greatly appreciated!

Thank you and good luck!